NEW TEACHERS HANDBOOK

No matter what your preparation has been to become a teacher, all teachers—new and experienced alike—agree that once you set foot into your classroom you need all the help and support you can get. And, what better way for new teachers to access that support than by learning from experienced teachers.

Forty-five teachers in our network contributed to the *New Teachers Handbook*, all eager for you to benefit from their expertise and experience. They have "been there," and this is the type of resource—*written by teachers, for teachers*—they wished they had in those first few incredibly challenging years. They are all routing for you to succeed and, in this spirit, are offering you their words of wisdom and tried and true practice.

Congratulations on becoming a teacher. Welcome to a profession in which you will have the opportunity to make a truly important contribution to society. To help you do that we invite you to dog-ear the pages that follow, write in the margins, and "take an idea and go creative." Good luck!

» Sponsor's Statement

We, at Philip Morris Companies Inc., are pleased to make this publication possible. With the overwhelming number of new teachers entering the profession, we all know the importance and the value of training. The **New Teachers Handbook** helps prepare teachers for their challenging new assignments with practical information and suggestions. Published by IMPACT II—The Teachers Network, the handbook is written by experienced classroom teachers expressly for new teachers.

Today's teacher operates in a highly complex environment. At the same time, there is an increasing need to help students thrive in an environment of diversity and learn from a wide array of role models —parents and teachers—in an atmosphere of tolerance, acceptance, and opportunity.

Recognizing these challenges and training opportunities, Philip Morris focuses its support for education on teachers and parents as primary agents of change in American education. This commitment to the future of our education system is in three areas:

» *recruiting and supporting new teachers, particularly people of color and non-traditional college students, such as older adults;*

» *preparing, supporting, and retaining new classroom teachers; and*

» *linking schools and parents.*

For more than four decades, the Philip Morris family of companies has contributed to education causes in communities throughout the United States. Today, Philip Morris is recognized as a leading corporate sponsor of teacher recruitment and training programs, and one of the top supporters of education in America.

Both IMPACT II and Philip Morris believe that schools will offer students a quality education only when they have the best prepared teachers. With school districts expected to hire more than 2,000,000 teachers in the next decade, the quality of education in our nation's schools will depend on the training and support that these newly hired teachers receive.

Through our support for teachers, Philip Morris and IMPACT II are helping to ensure that our schools are staffed with the best prepared and trained teachers. We applaud the veteran teachers who contributed their knowledge and expertise to the handbook. And, we welcome the new teachers to what we hope is the start of productive and rewarding new careers.

Stephanie French
Vice President
Corporate Contributions and Cultural Programs

contents

From Start to Finish:
A Strategic Plan

» The First Day:
Setting the tone for your classroom

The first day of school is often the most stressful both for you and your students. It is a big transition, and you have all been anticipating this day for a long time. You can make a good first impression by meeting each of your students at the door with a smile, a greeting, or a handshake. It's a small gesture, but it will go a long way towards setting a friendly and respectful atmosphere in your classroom. In order to begin to form a positive learning relationship, students need to feel genuine concern from their teacher. Research suggests that in the first weeks of the school year, the die is cast for the development of student self-esteem for the rest of the year, so let your students feel their importance to you as their teacher and your excitement about teaching them.

Students can "read" teachers instantly, so do not try to hide your lack of experience. Be honest. Tell them that this is your first teaching job, that you are beginning an adventure together, and that you may make mistakes but you will always be open to discussion. Learn the students' names quickly, and make sure they learn yours. Name tags, desktop name cards, seating charts, roll books, and name games can help in the beginning.

One of the first things that you will want to establish with your students is what you expect from them in terms of classroom behavior. Keep the rules simple, make the consequences logical and fair, and above all, be consistent from the very beginning in your enforcement of the rules. Empathy and caring, two essential ingredients of a working relationship, are transmitted not only through verbal communication, but through the way you manage your classroom on a daily basis.

It is especially important to plan your first day carefully. Choose at least one activity that involves the students in working together and getting to know a little about each other. You may want to share information about your own background that would be interesting to the students: other jobs you have held, places you have lived or visited, your family, your interests. One thing that will be helpful to you in many ways is having your students fill out questionnaires indicating their interests, hobbies, favorite and least favorite subjects, and any other information that they want to share with you.

It is important for you to know what really interests and excites your students, as this knowledge will enable you to design more engaging activities, and prepare you to handle various classroom issues that arise.

» Recognizing problems

Students are individuals with individual needs. Find the time to figure out what is going on in their lives. Often, a brief conversation can shed light on a particular problem. If you have difficulty finding out what's going on, ask a colleague who might have a relationship with that student.

Make it a priority to know your students' health status and anything else about them that could impede progress in school. Check their health records, ask for information during parent conferences, and consult with the school medical personnel.

In the process of getting to know your students, you may discover some problems that exceed the assistance that you can render at the classroom level. Is there help available? An emphatic YES! Begin your search with available school resources. At the onset of the year, most schools provide orientation printouts, and/or a handbook on available services. Use the handbook; become familiar with its contents. You may want to read reference materials that can assist you in understanding student problems. Conference with other teachers, the school administration, and the support staff—counselor, psychologist, therapist. Identify community agencies that can be of assistance. Prior to utilizing out-of-school contacts, however, be sure to obtain authorization from the school administrator. Also, you will need to telephone or meet with a parent or legal guardian to obtain permission and support.

» Strategic planning

Planning, both long-term and short-term, is absolutely essential to the smooth operation of your classroom. You must set goals for yourself and your students, but you should also be prepared to adjust those goals as you come to understand the needs and abilities of your students.

Study your district standards and the curriculum guides of your school. You will need to have a clear idea of where you want your students to be at the end of the year before you can begin your planning. Draw up a general outline for the year. If you are following a textbook, you might want to plot the approximate number of chapters you hope to cover each quarter, keeping in mind that the first chapters of a book are often review chapters that can be covered quickly, while the last chapters may require more time. If you are working from several sources, establishing a structure is even more important. Try to plan in terms of two-to-four week units. In addition to really acquainting yourself with any texts you will be using, you should consider which skills the students need to master first in order to move on to more complex challenges.

Once you have mapped out a general outline for the year, you can focus on what you want to accomplish during the first quarter, which will encompass about nine weeks. Keep in mind that you need a cushion of a few periods each quarter for unexpected interruptions—days when you will not teach, fire drills, and early dismissals due to weather conditions. It is helpful to use a semester or full-year planning grid with large blocks to write in (a calendar works well) when you schedule your units. Choose assessment days for both your own assessments and district-mandated tests, mark holidays and vacations, and factor in field trips, assemblies, and any other special events that might reduce the amount of time that you will spend on your regular teaching program. Consider the time required to grade major projects and tests, and if you are teaching more than one class, avoid having all of your students take tests or hand in essays on the same day. You can protect your personal life and insure yourself the free time you need by planning carefully.

Once you have established manageable goals for the quarter, you can plot out your lessons for the first few weeks. Your lesson plans should cover no less than two weeks' work. Avoid planning on a daily basis. There are two reasons for this. First, biweekly planning gives you an overall picture of where you are heading, and you can communicate this to your students. You need to have a clear sense of direction in order to maintain a healthy learning environment in your classroom. Students are quick to sense that a teacher doesn't know what he/she is doing. Second, it is easier and less nerve-wracking to do your planning once every two weeks. You can always revise as you go along.

Most students, not to mention parents, really appreciate a written calendar that lays out your weekly or biweekly plans. You can include homework assignments, books, or other materials they should bring to class, and announcements about future due dates. You might also want to clue students in on your daily plans by writing your goal or focus, along with any homework assignments, on the board before they arrive.

›› Planning lessons

There are several types of lessons (e.g. direct instruction, problem-based learning, discovery), various ways to arrange your students (e.g. individuals, cooperative groups, whole class), and myriad ways to put topics together with activities to create learning opportunities.

Our advice to new teachers is to take the traditional lesson plan format as a starting point and develop your own variations on it. Though it may seem like an unnecessary exercise, experienced teachers agree that putting your lesson objectives into words will help you to fine-tune your activities for each class. Keep your destination in sight when you are designing your lesson. Sometimes you can get away with a nifty activity and no real instructional goal beyond doing the nifty activity, but when these lessons go awry, they are painful and stressful. They can

THE FIRST HOMEWORK ASSIGNMENT

You can use the first homework assignment of the school year to provide your students with more information about you and your goals for the class, and to get some useful information about them. One veteran teacher writes a survival manual for her students, which playfully outlines her plans and expectations, and serves as the text for the first few days of school. Their first homework assignment, a writing activity, is explained in the manual.

"My objectives with this activity are several: to see if the kids really read the manual; to garner samples of the students' writing; to have some fun with the kids; and to determine how they solve problems.

"Always hoping to tap children's ingenuity, my first assignment gives students an opportunity to invent some pretty good excuses for not handing in their homework. The range of creative thinking delights me:

 5 ‹‹

∗ Believe it or not I actually finished my homework but then my mom thought that it was a letter to her friend and she sent it in today's mail. (DUSTIN)

∗ My homework isn't here on time because I was up all night thinking of a rhyme. I fell asleep, and to my dismay, an alien flew in and took it away. (CINDY)

"Aliens and over-zealous mothers seem to take the brunt of the blame for missing homework, though I have also concluded that family pets turn contrary at the start of the school year!"

LESSON PLANS

We encourage you to find your own way with lesson plans; however, know the traditional format:

AIM—the focus for the lesson, preferably stated in a question.

INSTRUCTIONAL OBJECTIVE—what students will know/be able to do at the end of the lesson.

DO NOW—a five-minute written activity to focus students on the lesson's aim.

MOTIVATION—a question that connects the lesson to the lives of the students.

TRANSITION—a sentence that explains how the teacher is moving from the motivation to the next part of the lesson.

PIVOTAL QUESTIONS—six-to-eight well thought-out questions that guide the discussion or activity.

APPLICATION—a homework assignment in which the students apply the knowledge or skill learned in the lesson.

leave the teacher paralyzed, frustrated, or at war with the kids. Well thought-out objectives can help you plan high quality lessons that are flexible enough to allow you to adapt on the spot, and to cover more ground in less time. When formulating your daily objectives, think in behavioral terms—not in terms of what your students will know, but of how they will be able to demonstrate their knowledge. Ask yourself which structures you can use to best facilitate, support, and assess their learning. Find a colleague you respect and watch how he/she plans lessons. Ask a lot of questions. Invite this colleague to look at your plans and visit your classroom. Above all, trust your gut when it comes to lesson planning. Be true to yourself, and find the structures that work best for you and your students.

"One opening activity that works well for me is duplicating a short text and asking each student to annotate it, then pass it along to the student to the right, and respond to any annotation made by the student to the left. This gives students an opportunity to help determine the starting points of the discussion. Once I see what they are thinking, I may come in the next day with a highly defined aim, but I don't want to skip over their thinking immediately to impose mine. Why? They never seem to get mine very well if I don't get theirs first. In the six years I've been teaching, I've learned the need for structure in a lesson, but I'm always searching for structures that allow students to help shape the classroom experience."

However you choose to structure your lesson, it is wise to plan for more than you will probably accomplish. If you do not need that "something extra," it will always be on the back burner as a possibility for another day.

One of the hardest aspects of first-year teaching is the lack of collected resources. Unlike veteran teachers, you cannot just reach into your files and pull out a successful activity. You must plan and create almost everything you do and that is definitely time consuming. The good news is, the hard work you put in now will serve you well for years to come. Remember that every September will be easier than the one before it.

REACH BEYOND THE WALLS OF YOUR CLASSROOM

Children love to play with new technology, and they are naturals when it comes to discovering original applications. You can take them far beyond the walls of your classroom, school, and community by teaching them the language of technology and helping them develop the flexibility to adapt to its uses. Here are some tips from experienced teachers:

* Teach your students how and when to use the Internet to research topics.
* Open a class e-mail account so that your students can communicate with experts besides teachers and parents.
* Show students how to take snapshots in the field with a digital video camera and then print the images or load them onto web pages. The camera can also function as a videoconferencing tool.
* Use a scanner to import artwork and to load students' drawings onto web pages.
* Don't forget about the good old "low tech" devices, such as telephones and tape recorders, which many students are not accustomed to incorporating into their research.

By teaching students to use new technologies effectively, you can both empower them as individuals and demonstrate the value of teamwork and cooperation. By providing them with ways to conduct original research inexpensively, you encourage them to become problem solvers. Finally, by helping your students establish contact with people outside of their school and community, you enable them to become productive citizens of the world.

›› Managing time

As a new teacher, you will be juggling an enormous range of new responsibilities, from writing lesson plans and devising a grading system to designing bulletin boards and learning school procedures. It will often feel like there are simply not enough hours in a day. Time management is a serious issue for beginning educators; teaching is exhausting, so you can't afford to skimp on sleep to get everything done. What follows is a list of time management tips offered by experienced teachers:

1. WORK WITH YOUR TEACHER AIDES AND PARENT VOLUNTEERS. If you are lucky, you may have a teacher aide available to assist you occasionally. Aides can accomplish many routine but important tasks for you, such as tallying attendance records, grading papers or notebooks, filling out report cards, calling parents, updating student records, and dealing with book orders. Keep an ongoing list on your desk of possible jobs that the aide can do for you when he/she has free time. Parent volunteers often enjoy being given specific tasks to do as well.

TECHNOLOGY-BASED LESSON PLANS

It is easy to say that teachers should integrate technology into their lesson plans, but it is not so easy to do. First and foremost, it requires that you, the teacher, really familiarize yourself with the available technology. It is also important that you choose or design activities that meet your curriculum goals and reinforce the academic skills that you want your students to master. One of the exciting things about technology-based lesson plans is that they often involve more than one subject area and can give students a chance to exercise a range of skills.

Oscar De La Renta, Take Notes!

This lesson is designed as a culminating activity for a climate study unit.

CONTENT AREAS: Social Studies/ Geography/ Communication Arts

INSTRUCTIONAL OBJECTIVE: Students will be able to identify world climate regions and demonstrate their understanding by designing appropriate fashions for the various climate zones.

MATERIALS:
  * Presentation software
  * Scanner
  * Audio recorder

MOTIVATION: Students have been taught about the various climate zones, from tropical to arctic. What better way to help them retain these ideas than to have them create fashions that are appropriate for the different climates. Each student can create an outfit for a male and a female from a particular region, and for different seasons if necessary. The project will culminate in a computer-generated fashion show.

PROCEDURE:
1. The teacher picks four locations in different climate zones. For example: Lagos, Nigeria (tropical wet/dry); Ontario, Canada (humid continental); Siberia (tundra/polar); Phoenix, Arizona (semi-arid).
2. The students are split up so that all of the

climate zones are covered. Each student is expected to design a line of clothing—for kids or working adults—appropriate for one of the zones.

3. The designs must reflect clothing that can be worn year-round. If there are four seasons in the zone, students choose two seasons to design for.

4. Students can use a scanner to scan pictures into the computer and edit them in a drawing program. They can also use the drawing tools to design clothing and accessories directly on the computer.

5. Students use presentation software to insert designs into consecutive slides.

6. Students create "runway narratives" describing the fashions, and use an audio recorder to record them. The narrative should include vivid descriptions of the styles and fabrics, and explain why they are appropriate for the particular climate region. The descriptions can include background music.

7. A projection device is used to present each student's fashion show to the class. (If a projection device is unavailable, students can gather around a computer, a few at a time, to watch and judge the fashion show.)

EVALUATION: Students should set criteria for evaluation that include both the appeal and appropriateness of the fashions for the climate region, and the quality of the presentation itself. Was the narration accurate? Were vivid descriptors used? Was music incorporated? If so, how did it affect the presentation?

2. MAKE LESSON PLANS WORK FOR YOU. Well-organized lesson plans can save you a lot of time. You can schedule certain assignments and assessments for days when you think your work load will be lighter, or when you have a teacher aide at your disposal to help with the grading. Also, if you plan units well in advance, you can make copies all at once and have your materials ready when you need them.

3. PUT YOUR STUDENTS TO WORK. Keep a job list and let your students help you run the classroom efficiently. Also, certain types of work can be graded or checked over by your students. It's no crime to correct an assignment in class. It's an excellent teaching opportunity, as students can ask questions, and teachers have a chance to reteach or reinforce certain concepts.

4. DO SOME GRADING AND/OR PLANNING EVERY DAY. You might want to come in a half-hour early or leave a half-hour late. A little prep time on a regular basis can make a real difference in your outlook and presentation. This also means making the most of your planning period. However, prep periods are often eaten up with meetings and social visits, signing out equipment, or calling parents, and are not really reliable as grading time. Don't allow yourself to fall behind as a result of depending on prep periods for grading. A huge pile of ungraded work can be depressing and really eat into your evening and weekend time.

5. BE HONEST WITH STUDENTS. If you are drowning in research papers, explain to them how thorough you are trying to be and how long it takes you to grade each one. They will understand.

6. SAVE TIME NEXT YEAR TOO. Buy or beg a set of manila file folders. Save everything that you create for lessons this year. Label the folders specifically so you can locate the materials easily in a year, and put them in your file cabinet. Rubrics, duplicated materials, puzzles, answer keys, worksheets, creative lesson plans, assessments, and evaluation sheets can all be reused. With minor alterations, one of this year's successful lessons can be reproduced for next year's class.

Just remember, there is only one first year! It will be a struggle but you will survive, and you will learn an enormous amount. Be confident that with a little practice you will find a way to get everything done and still have time to do the things that are important to you outside of school.

Classroom
Management

"The secret of education lies in respecting the pupil."
— Ralph Waldo Emerson

A well-managed classroom is an environment in which students know what is expected of them, materials are stimulating and accessible, and teaching methods are appropriate to the students' learning styles and needs. Successful management also depends on your ability as a teacher to recognize, interpret and respond to the events that occur daily in your classroom. The most effective teachers actively organize their time, space, materials, auxiliary personnel, and students to create and maintain an environment that is truly conducive to learning.

"I start off the school year by setting the stage for a natural human relationship with all students. Initial activities involve the children in creating this kind of environment. First, all students complete an interest inventory to determine special interests, likes and dislikes, strengths and weaknesses. This becomes the first entry in student folders that I keep on file for use throughout the year. As we begin to learn about each other as individuals, I ask the students to think of all the ways our classroom could be made into the best possible place for learning. All ideas are noted and discussed to determine which should be adapted to our classroom setting. I find that this activity leads naturally into our determining a set of conduct guidelines that all students must use to reach our goal for the kind of classroom we want to establish and maintain."

Though it may seem unimportant alongside all the other issues you have to consider at the beginning of the year, if you want your classroom to run smoothly, you will need to give some careful thought to the establishment of basic classroom procedures. Students will need to leave your classroom to go to the bathroom, the nurse, the office, and other parts of the building. How do you want papers turned in? What about homework? What should students do when they enter your classroom? What kind of headings should they put on their papers? How should they participate in a class discussion? Do you expect them to keep the classroom neat? Each year, students are confronted with new teachers and new rules. Take the time you need to explain and practice all procedures right off the bat, so your precious class time can be spent on more important things.

>> Designing a creative learning environment

It is important that students feel comfortable and relaxed in the classroom, which should represent a "safe haven" of sorts, while sparking curiosity and excitement. Decorate your classroom in a way that gives you pleasure while encouraging students to participate in the development of their environment. Leave places to hang student-generated work and update this frequently. You might want to have students volunteer to make bulletin boards, murals, or other curriculum-generated displays. A well-designed classroom can also motivate students by providing various learning centers where they can engage in interesting activities, either in small groups or individually, when their required work is finished.

You will want to give careful thought to choosing a seating arrangement. There are times when students need to focus on the teacher, blackboard, or overhead projector. On the other hand, you will often be working together as a class and you want your students to be able to see each other and communicate comfortably without rearranging their desks. For certain activities you may have students work in pairs or small groups, or get up and circulate to other parts of the room.

One seating arrangement that is flexible enough to address all the needs of an active classroom is the configuration of two concentric horseshoes with the openings toward the front of the room. This arrangement is equally effective for large and small classes. The inner horseshoe should always be filled first, so the teacher is as close as possible to the students, and no one has the opportunity to sit alone in the back of the room and disengage from the class. The configuration allows students to interact and work easily with those next to them, across the room, immediately behind, or in front of them.

"All the possibilities of the double-horseshoe configuration reinforce my deepest beliefs about my teaching: that my role is that of a guide or coach; that students need both security and challenge; and that they learn best from each other."

If you have assigned seats in any configuration, it is healthy to rotate the class every couple of weeks: have each student move over a few places, remaining seated next to the same students but in a different part of the room. These shifts prevent students from laying claim to any particular position—close to the door, facing the door, the back of the room, or the front—while allowing them the security of sitting next to the same people. The practice of shifting also prevents teachers from developing conscious or unconscious patterns of calling on certain students because they are seated in positions that make it easier to see or hear them.

Whatever seating arrangement works best for you, it is important to explain your expectations of the configuration to your students. Even if the configuration is the same in every classroom, different teachers will place different expectations on it, so students will find it helpful to hear exactly what you are looking for.

"I want my students to give each other information and encouragement, to focus on the topic at hand, and to listen to each other and to me; so I make all those expectations as clear as I can. In the first few weeks of class, some students see my seating arrangement as tacit permission to ignore me or others, or to signal to friends across the room. But after a few weeks I usually find that some students have understood and internalized my expectations to a point where they explain them to other students—and that point marks the beginning of our classroom community."

≫ Empowering students

Part of being a creative teacher is using strategies and resources to empower your students. This can be as simple as trusting students to run errands, grade papers, or operate a duplicating machine, and it can do wonders for their self-esteem. When you find yourself running around in a frenzy while the students are just sitting there, waiting for materials or for the next activity to begin, stop and ask yourself how you can achieve the same goals with the students participating in the work. They will learn from all phases of an activity, including getting it set up and organized. Many teachers have found that assigning regular classroom jobs builds a sense of camaraderie in the classroom and helps students with issues of responsibility.

"My students were thrilled with the idea of jobs—pets, plants/garden, and computers being three of the most popular jobs. Through the process of brainstorming, 11 jobs were selected and job descriptions decided upon. The class decided that these jobs would be rotated weekly among my 27 students. The 11 jobs were: pets, plants/garden, computers, recycling, messenger, librarian, attendance, mail, board/overhead, book orders, and materials. The attendance person not only checks on who is present, but fills out a "While You Were Gone" form for the student(s) absent, and includes worksheets that were given out that day and the results of any class meeting. Through these routine responsibilities, many of the students have learned new skills, such as gardening and computer maintenance, and passed those skills on to other students."

≫ Coping with classroom size and composition

Although classroom composition is largely determined by the social, economic, and educational structure of the community, and the number of students per class is often dictated by the school district in which a teacher is employed, there are a few basic management skills that can be applied under most conditions. Class size may vary. Teachers need to be well-prepared to educate large numbers, often without auxiliary personnel. Teachers also need to coordinate and implement educational programs to serve students from diverse ability levels, as well as varied racial and ethnic backgrounds. How can these seemingly impossible tasks be accomplished?

First and foremost, the classroom teacher must be confident and optimistic in face of each new challenge, and transfer these feelings to the students. The more confident you feel in your knowledge of your students, curriculum, teaching methods, and discipline procedures, the more successful your educational program is likely to be. When planning your lessons, rely on as much educational data and background information about the class as possible. This information may be obtained from test results, interest inventories, cumulative records, discussions with other teachers, and interviews with students. Identifying similarities and differences among students can help you accomplish a maximum number of learning objectives within given time constraints, as this will allow you to vary your teaching techniques according to your students' needs, and group students in the ways that are most conducive to learning. Recognizing the similarities and differences between your students is also essential to teaching young people in a multicultural society. Each student will learn better if he/she feels that his/her own culture or heritage is recognized and appreciated in an open, inclusive classroom atmosphere. Creating a respectful and trusting community begins with sharing and learning from all students in your classroom.

Make an effort to provide classroom activities that foster positive relationships, both between you and the individual students, and among the students themselves. Small-group and peer-teaching activities will help students learn to work cooperatively. All students should be actively engaged in the learning process—not just high-ability students. Developing warm and positive relationships will motivate the whole class to learn.

» Maintaining discipline

The establishment of rules is one of the first steps to managing a classroom efficiently. Students are more likely to follow rules if they have participated in developing them. The following guidelines should be helpful:

* Limit the number of rules; five or six positive ones are usually sufficient.
* Solicit students' ideas and suggestions for consideration as rules.
* Design rules that enhance student learning.
* State the rules in language that the students understand.
* Determine in advance the consequences of keeping or breaking the rules.
* Print, display, distribute, and sign contracted rules with the students.

"At the beginning of the year—on the very first day, and then each day of the first week—I establish the expectations I have for my students. I make them realistic, sensible, and fair. I test students for their understanding of these rules as I would for any other information."

An effective classroom management system should provide opportunities for group discussion. You may want to use class meetings or discussion groups to obtain students' opinions on specific topics or problems. Your role at these discussion sessions should be that of guide, moderator, and arbitrator.

"Throughout the year as problems arise, I rely on the classroom meeting discussion strategy to help the class determine changes and improvements that need to be made. Classroom meeting rules are established and agreed upon by the total group before discussion begins:

1. **Everyone sits in a circle in order to be seen and heard easily.**
2. **The president of the class or the teacher opens the meeting by stating the area of concern.**
3. **One person speaks at a time. Each student has the right to be heard. No talking or whispering is allowed. Any student causing a disturbance will be asked to leave the circle.**
4. **The first time around the circle, everyone can have input on the topic. The second time around, suggestions are made to solve the problem or make changes.**
5. **The class secretary keeps notes on suggestions made, so that a final decision based on consensus can be reached.**

"The classroom-meeting strategy enables students to learn to respect each other's ideas, to lis-

ten, and to make decisions that affect the individual as well as the group. It also develops a sense of commitment to the goals that were established during the first weeks of school. Students can learn to accept responsibility for their actions and abide by the decisions they have made."

Disruptive behavior will be minimized, and learning enhanced if students are encouraged to interact positively and support one another's efforts. To maintain a friendly but task-oriented classroom atmosphere, it may be helpful to grade more than just written work. For example, when a student gives an oral presentation the other students could be graded on their listening skills. Points may be deducted if students talk during a presentation by another student. After a presentation, you might ask a student to repeat one fact he/she learned from the report, and another student to explain one thing he/she liked about the presentation. This also helps the speaker, who receives at least two positive comments before sitting down.

Unfortunately, every classroom has one—or several—students who provoke negative attention. They seem to set up situations that elicit constant responses from you. Try to play up positive behavior with attention-demanders:

"A few years ago, I began using index cards to communicate with these students, politely asking them to refrain from... or begin working on..., always ending it with, 'I'll help you if you need it.' Amazingly, the students complied with my written requests. I felt as if I had discovered a magic wand. I carried it further. When a student improved in some way, I'd write a personal note as a compliment and casually drop it on the student's desk. More than once, I have seen an 'incorrigible' retrieve my note from a jacket pocket to reread several times during the class period. One young man even asked me if he could show the note to his mother and probation officer!"

» Grouping options

Students respond best to variety when it comes to teaching techniques, so try to vary your methods from the teacher-directed class—where you are the center of attention, to peer-group learning, to individual projects. There is no single best approach to the grouping of students for instructional purposes. Large groups, small groups, and one-on-one pairings are each appropriate at given times. Grouping, in and of itself, is not a panacea for education. What the teacher does with the curriculum within a particular setting will determine how successful the students are in learning.

How often you use groups depends on how comfortable you are with the concept. Some teachers use groups sparingly or not at all, while others use them almost exclusively. Students tend to love group work because it is enjoyable and stimulating for them to work with their peers. It also gives them a chance to engage in a different type of learning process.

If you think you are going to be using groups during the year, it is probably best to have a group project, such as a reading/writing group roundtable or a study group, in place fairly soon after school starts, just to set the tone. The easiest way to start groups is simply to count off students as they are seated in the classroom, making groups out of the first four, the second four, and so on. This has the added advantage of letting the kids get acquainted with students they may not know. The two main things you need to stress clearly are: 1) what they are to accomplish, and 2) what each group member's responsibility is. You can assign specific

Behavior Contracts: One Teacher's Experience

Occasionally, every teacher encounters a student who simply does not respond to the usual methods of classroom management, or who has special needs that require a more intensive, individualized approach. Behavior contracts have been used with particularly disruptive students with a very high degree of success. A behavior contract is just that, a contract between a student and teacher—written out, clearly defined, and signed by all involved parties. A behavior contract works best when it targets a very specific, definable problem that can be evaluated within a fairly short unit of time—daily or even hourly.

"I could tell from the first day that R. was going to be a challenge. He was openly defiant and delighted in interfering with the learning of other students. He would hide or destroy their work, distract them in class, and encourage others to emulate his behavior. The first thing I needed to figure out was what kind of incentive would work for this student. Luckily, I had given all of my students an interest inventory on the first day of school, just to find out more about them. When I reread his inventory, I quickly saw that this student valued one activity above all others—basketball.

"The next step was to talk with him honestly about my frustrations, to tell him exactly what my expectations were, and to find out if he was interested in improving his behavior and doing better in school. He said that he would like to do better in school, so we worked out a contract and went over it together.

"We came up with two target behaviors that would be evaluated four times a day. The first was following directions with regard to classroom assignments without a defiant attitude. For this behavior he could receive one reminder per evaluation period and still succeed. The second was to stop disrupting the work of other students and to stop encouraging others to do the same. He was allowed no reminders for this behavior.

"He was responsible for keeping his contract and marking yes or no for each period. He was also required to have the contract initialed, either by me or by one of his other teachers, after each of his self-evaluations. If he forgot to fill it out or to obtain the teacher's initials, it counted as a no. If he was successful four out of five days a week, he would earn his reward, which was to play basketball with me for 15 or 20 minutes after school on Friday. This was something he really wanted, and that, coupled with the responsibility of keeping his own contract, was all it took to turn him around. After a couple of months, he no longer needed the contract and we phased it out, but we continued to play basketball every Friday afternoon."

tasks to specific group members, or let the group decide who will do what. Inform the groups of their objectives, the constraints, and procedures. The students should function independently, with the teacher acting as a facilitator, consulted by a group member only after the group has tested all possible problem-solving resources. Group evaluation questionnaires to be filled out by all students at the completion of the project will help keep every student involved and productive.

After you know the students better and have more of an understanding of what each one is capable of, you might want to group them according to their skills, being careful to vary the groups both in size and ability mix. If you have pairs working together on spelling, for example, pair a poor speller with a good speller one time, and the next time pair a good speller with another good speller. It is not a bad idea to put two weaker students together once in a while; they will often feel more comfortable and work to help one another. When you organize groups of four, you might want to try putting two weaker students with two stronger students; that way the stronger students are each challenged by someone equally strong, and the weaker students benefit from the stronger students' help without feeling outnumbered. It is also a good idea to let students choose their own groups once in a while. The easiest way to do this is to post a sign-up sheet divided into groups of four.

COOPERATIVE LEARNING

Cooperative learning teams are not the same as small groups. Cooperative learning is a much more structured, long-term approach to group work, which requires a higher level of up-front preparation on the part of the teacher, and more practice on the part of the students. Over a thousand studies have indicated that this technique is highly effective in improving academic achievement, self-esteem, and discipline, but it takes time to work out the kinks. It may take several weeks for your classroom to run smoothly with a cooperative learning system, but it will give you time for the rest of the year. The basic idea is that kids work in teams. The teams are made up of a mix of talents and each student has a specific role to play in the group.

The method is composed of five essential elements: interdependence, individual accountability, direct teaching of social skills, self evaluation or processing, and interaction. Each member assumes responsibility for his/her own learning, as well as for the progress of all members in the group. Direct teaching of social skills includes strategies for developing and maintaining leadership, decision making, trust, communication, and conflict management. Self-evaluation involves students in evaluating the extent to which the various objectives of the lesson were accomplished. Interaction is ensured by the seating arrangement, in which students are facing each other and influencing each other's thinking and social skills.

The role of the teacher is very important in cooperative learning. Whereas in traditional instruction the teacher is more of a lecturer and tends to dominate the lesson, in cooperative learning the teacher acts as a facilitator who specifies objectives, makes decisions about the composition of groups, explains the task to be completed, creates positive interdependence, monitors and intervenes to teach social and collaborative skills, and evaluates achievement and group effectiveness. In setting up the groups, you must be careful to mix students of diverse backgrounds and ethnic groups. In time, strong friendships and an understanding of differences will often develop. Experienced teachers have found that cooperative learning is rewarding on many levels, as the best learning takes place when students teach one another and promote each other's progress.

INDEPENDENT PROJECTS

Every class subject lends itself, at one time or another, to independent projects. Tasks or activities can be designed for all ability levels, and made available for student selection. You may find Bloom's Taxonomy a useful resource as you work to design projects for all learning levels. Tasks can be written to address skills at the lowest level (knowledge) or the highest level (evaluation), so that all students can successfully complete projects appropriate to their abilities and interests. Present and discuss guidelines for the completion of independent projects with your students before you initiate the assignment. When the projects are finished, make sure you give the students a chance to share their work with each other.

"My students do a great deal of writing, including journal entries, learning logs, and discussion responses, which I share orally. I carefully choose five papers which cover as many different ability levels as possible. I read all five to the class, then ask the five 'authors' to pick up their papers, which I have ceremoniously placed on the front table. The class does not know which student wrote which paper, unless the writer wants them to know. I have heard comments like, 'I didn't think he ever did any work,' or 'If she can write like that, then I know I can,' or the truly rewarding, 'I really like your story. You are a good writer.' I love to hear my students compliment each other."

PEER TUTORING

Peer tutoring is another management system that promotes student achievement. It provides an opportunity for students who have mastered the material to share their knowledge and practice their skills, while giving you time to work with the students who really need your individual attention. An effectively organized peer tutoring program will help you manage your classroom more efficiently.

No matter how hard you try, no matter how many different methods you use to get your lesson across, some students are just not going to get it. Others will struggle until they halfway understand, and feel frustrated when they have to concentrate on something else as you move on to the next lesson. It is helpful to call on other students to assist at this stage. Other kids can often relate to the problem and explain things in terms that the faltering student can understand.

You can use peer tutoring on a fairly informal basis in your classroom whenever you sense that your class is split between those who understand and those who are still struggling. Simply designate "helpers" who are excused from a particular assignment but who move around the class offering to help those who are working on the assignment. These helpers can be given a badge to wear, or their names can be written on the board. This frees you to help the students having the greatest difficulty, and provides the borderline students with some individual attention from students you know have mastered a particular skill.

Another way to use peer tutors is in a more formal situation, where the tutor gets

A good way to introduce the process of cooperative learning to your students is to hand out an information sheet that provides them with a clear overview of the process and addresses some of the
questions and reservations that they typically have. The information sheet can serve as a springboard
for discussion, and it also gives the students something to refer to when questions arise later on. The
following example might give you some ideas:

GROUPIES "R" US
—A student information sheet for long-term group projects

WHY DO WE WORK IN GROUPS?
Research shows that of all the learning styles, cooperative learning has the greatest long-term effect
and supplies unlimited benefits for the classroom as well as the individual student. You may have had
negative experiences working in groups before. You may have been in groups where other individuals
did not do their jobs or did their jobs poorly and you ended up doing more than your share of the work.
This type of experience can make students hesitant to jump into another round of group work, but by
building the basis for successful groups, these concerns can be addressed.

HOW DO WE ORGANIZE A SUCCESSFUL GROUP?
1. It's a misconception that everyone in every group will do the same amount of work. That is simply not true. Sometimes you will do the most work, and sometimes others will have to carry you. Be
honest with your group about what you can and cannot accomplish. Remember that each group member has strengths and weaknesses.

2. Always work from a calendar (start at the due date and work backwards), assign each member
specific duties and a date when his/her work is due, and keep a careful record of who has turned in
what. Do not accept late work more than once!

3. If your group is not functioning, ask the teacher to sit down and help resolve the conflict. If you
really want to resolve problems, when you talk with your group, use the word "I" and stay away from
the word "you," which can often lead to accusations. A student who is not working successfully in a
given group has the option of completing the work on his/her own, or possibly joining another group.

4. Make all final copies of your group work due at least one day before the final due date, so you
have time to review and work on any weak areas.

Group work is an essential life skill. Studies show, for example, that employers are more interested in
hiring people who can work effectively with others. The skills you gain in group work will be useful to
you for the rest of your life, in ways you can't even imagine.

together with his/her assigned student either during class or after school. You might want to offer extra credit for providing such help.

You can usually find tutors in upper grades for students who are really struggling, either through the honor society or through other teachers. You may find an advanced placement teacher who is amenable to allowing some of his/her students to come into your class and help groups or individuals. Do not be afraid to ask. Many teachers will be honored, and the students who help almost always respond enthusiastically and seriously to the task at hand.

Most of us learned by the lecture method, but that is only one way to get information across to a group of people in a short period of time. There are as many ways beyond lecturing to teach content and skills as there are different ways to learn. Learning styles will vary widely within a classroom, which is why it is so important to vary your teaching style. By developing a repertoire of teaching strategies, you can tap into the natural learning styles of all of your students.

Suggestion Box

Here are a few classroom tips that other teachers have found effective:

✳ Create a message pocket for each student—library pockets or envelopes work well— to encourage writing and social skills. You can use these to communicate with individual students, and the students can write to each other.

✳ Photocopy pictures of students and use them for labeling lockers, message pockets, author pages, etc.

✳ Instead of having to scribble out passes for nurse, library, office, and bathroom, cut one-inch dowels about four to six inches long. Drill a small hole in one end, and string with colored yarn. Write with waterproof ink the type of pass each dowel is to be used for, and hang these passes in a spot close to the door. It will save you a lot of time.

10 Insights into Developing a Productive Career in Education *by Wayne Carlson*

During my 30+ years as a professional educator—a teacher—I have faced many challenges and have had many incredible experiences. I have taught American history to Navajo Indians in a Bureau of Indian Affairs boarding school in Utah, and world geography to the children of nuclear physicists in Los Alamos, New Mexico. For the past 18 years, I have taught social studies in Brush, a small rural community on the Great Plains of Eastern Colorado. Most of my experience has been at the middle school level. I have come to the firm conclusion that what you teach is not nearly as important as how you teach. Kids don't really care what you know until they know that you care. I have had the privilege of having all three of my sons in my class and have had the opportunity to work with many wonderful people. I would like to share some of the insights that I have gained over the tenure of my career. I believe they are the keys to a productive career in education.

#1 **Be consistent.** Deliberate carefully about the rules that you want to establish in your classroom. Keep them simple and be prepared to follow through. The fewer rules you have, the fewer will be violated. Be clear about the consequences and never make threats unless you plan to carry them out, because someone will invariably test you. I have three rules in my classroom: 1) be on time, 2) be prepared for class, and 3) respect the rights of others.

#2 **Be creative.** Change directions frequently. Pretend that your classroom is a vehicle that has 24 gears. Use each and every one of them periodically. Variety truly is the spice of life. Kids like active learning. I believe the most effective way to learn is by making discoveries, and the best way to teach is to provide opportunities for these discoveries.

#3 **Be friendly.** I have found that I am the one who sets the tone for each of my classes. If I stand at the doorway and greet each student with a friendly and personal greeting, he/she treats me and the rest of the class differently than if I don't. Take the time to get to know at least a little bit about each of your students. I have nearly 140 students and I know this takes a great deal of time, but it is an invaluable investment. Be cheerful and friendly with your colleagues, even the ones that can be difficult to get along with. Take the initiative and go the extra mile to promote congenial relations, especially with the people with whom you work closely. It is equally important that you maintain good relationships with the administration and support staff. Many teachers look at the principal as "the Enemy" and treat him/her as such, which can become a self-fulfilling situation. Be positive, cooperative, and helpful. Make a special effort with the janitorial staff—they can make your life miserable if they don't like or respect you. Try to maintain good relationships on every level.

#4 **Utilize community resources.** Talk to parents at conferences and find out about their jobs, hobbies, and interests. Use resource people whenever you can. Get to know the education reporter from the local newspaper. Don't forget that the local library and/or museum is full of interesting resources. Take field trips into the community, and get to know as many local people as you can. Try to invite local people into your classroom on a regular basis. They will become your support system.

#5 **Be flexible.** I remember the day in my first year as a classroom teacher when my principal was due to visit for an "official observation." I had a dynamic lesson planned that would undoubtedly "knock his socks off." I had my anticipatory set, and my objectives, activities, and closure down pat. A key part of my lesson involved a short filmstrip (this was 30 years ago) and, wouldn't you know it, the bulb on the filmstrip projector went out! Fortunately, having been a classroom teacher himself, the principal understood the situation and I survived. Ever since, I have always kept an extra "bulb" on hand and have learned to roll with the punches. You can bet that sometime during your career, a lesson or activity that you consider absolutely essential will be messed up by a fire drill or some other eventuality, so be flexible and keep your cool.

#6 **Be involved.** Take an active role in your professional organization. Be a leader. Be an innovator. Let others walk in your shadow. Join the educational sorority. Get involved in your church. Join the local museum. I really believe that you get out of life what you put into it. Don't sit there and watch the parade pass you by. Grab a baton and jump on the bandwagon. Volunteer for as many things as your schedule will allow. I have personally been a leader in the effort to establish a local museum. I was elected to the initial board of directors of the Brush Area Museum and Cultural Center. I chaired a committee of local citizens who placed a marker commemorating the Texas Montana Cattle Trail, which passed through Brush during the late 1800s. I was primarily responsible for obtaining national historic designation for the school building that will soon house our museum. I met and got to know many wonderful local people whom I now use as resource people in my history classes. This was a wonderful experience for me and has made me a better teacher.

#7 **Continue your education.** Some of my most wonderful and most meaningful educational experiences have occurred during the last few years. I have taken groups of middle school kids to Washington D.C. for each of the last 10 summers. They love it and learn a great deal, but I have gained much more than any of them. The opportunity to meet new people and to see new things is incredible! Two summers ago I camped and lived with traditional Navajo people and experienced their culture. I even got to participate in a sweat ceremony at the bottom of Canyon de Chelley in Arizona—an opportunity few anglos get. This year I am planning to take a group of my students on an exchange program to visit these same wonderful people.

#8 **Interact with your colleagues.** You will be amazed at what a wonderful bunch of people you work with. At Brush Middle School we have a team of five teachers who teach the core subjects (reading, English, science, math, and social studies). We work together on a daily basis and share a common planning period. We really help each other to be the best we can be. We have developed several interdisciplinary units that help our students understand the ways in which different types of learning are connected. You may not like some of the people you work with, but it is important to realize that each one is an individual with many ideas that can make you a more effective teacher.

#9 Have fun! Sometimes your days will seem to pass so slowly that you will feel like the next vacation will never come. But when you get to the point in your career that I have reached, you will wonder what in the world happened. How could time possibly have gone by so quickly? My most important piece of advice to you is to have fun. Don't worry about the car payment. Be silly sometimes. Let your hair down. Act like a 13-year-old once in a while. My friend and colleague Ken and I play ping pong nearly every night after school for half an hour. We never talk about school or students. That is probably the most important time for each of us because we just relax and have a good time.

#10 You are important. The financial rewards of teaching school are not great. My oldest son is in his third year as an electrical engineer. I have taught for 30+ years. He makes more money than I do. But the intrinsic rewards of this profession are greater than any other. The chance to influence young lives like we do is an awesome privilege and a tremendous opportunity. I was recently reminded of that fact. Last fall I welcomed about 125 new seventh grade students into my classroom. Most of them were naturally a bit nervous about the new school year and all the new teachers. After a few days they realized that seventh grade was not going to be so bad and settled into the routine.

I had one student who was different from most. He was new to the community, new to the school, and was very shy and anxious. He was as cute as could be with freckles, dimples, and a cowlick. He could easily have passed for Tom Sawyer, or the Beaver. The only kids he knew were a group of bullies who had taken it upon themselves to "initiate" him and make his life generally miserable. He was relatively small and easy to intimidate. He was introverted, polite, and vulnerable. His name was Matt Brown. Matt was a very average student who had to work hard to achieve decent grades. He figured out quickly that in my room he was safe and that I could be his friend. He and I had a lot of common interests, especially collecting football and baseball cards. I started calling him Brownie (which he loved) and made sure he got lots of positive attention. Gradually the other students started viewing him differently, and he developed several friendships. Even the class bullies began to treat him decently. Throughout the year, Brownie and I developed a special relationship. He brought in his autographed John Elway card and I brought in my Brett Favre. When I was on lunch duty, he hung around and we talked about all kinds of things. Since his parents were divorced, I became one of his adult male role models. He became a happy, well-adjusted, "normal" middle school student with lots of friends. The last day of school, I received one of those invaluable intrinsic rewards that make teaching worthwhile. I received a letter from Matt's mom. It read:

Dear Mr. Carlson,

When my son Matt entered seventh grade at Brush Middle School this past fall, he was scared to death. He had no friends. He was being bullied and harassed unmercifully by a group of boys and absolutely hated school. Many mornings I literally had to force him out the door. Your classroom was a safe haven for him. When you started calling him "Brownie" and joking around with him in your class, he gradually became "one of the guys" and really started loosening up and making friends. Now he is ornery and happy and actually looks forward to going to school. Thank you so much for the way you helped "Brownie" fit in. I will forever be indebted to you.

Sincerely,
Linda Short

Aligning Standards, Curriculum, and Assessment

» Designing and implementing your classroom curriculum

What do we want our students to know when they leave our classrooms? What will they remember of all we tried to teach them? What skills will they need to become successful, productive citizens?

The teaching of factual knowledge is certainly not obsolete, but the challenge our schools now face is teaching students how to manage the amazing quantity of information that the world lays on their doorsteps. The skills that are needed include evaluating, analyzing, investigating, prioritizing, presenting, negotiating, persuading, planning, predicting, following directions, and managing time. If we are successful in teaching these skills, students will become lifelong learners, able to solve problems, work cooperatively, and thrive in an ever-changing global community.

The best thing you can do for your students is plan ahead. As you attempt to align curriculum, assessment, and instruction, begin by looking at the big picture and finding the overriding ideas set forth by your district's standards. This will lead you directly to the question, "How does it look when students get it?" By thinking about the end result and imagining various levels of proficiency, you begin to define your instructional goals. The process of defining the performance level that you want your students to achieve will help you fine tune your expectations for various stages of student learning and design appropriate assessment tools.

From the beginning, explain the lesson or unit objectives to your students and make it clear that their grades depend on meeting those objectives. Ideally, as the year progresses, you will involve students in setting individual and group objectives. A yearly or quarterly outline can provide the class with a framework and a feeling of shared responsibility for the learning process.

Throughout the planning and implementation of a given unit, flexibility—both in terms of timing and activity selection—is essential. Ask for and listen to feedback from students so that you can constantly reassess the effectiveness of your activities in helping students to meet the standards and achieve the assessment goals. You should assess them frequently with a diversity of instruments, as they will surprise you regularly, both with what they know and what they do not know. If you identify the problem areas, you can fix them. Be aware of which students have mastered the material so you can incorporate this wonderful resource into your teaching strategy, through peer tutoring or small-group activities. It can be as simple as carrying a clipboard and checking off which students know how to do long division or break down the parts of a sentence.

You should know exactly what you want your students to be able to demonstrate to you, show them what they should know how to do, and test them on the material you have made them responsible for. In this way you will provide them with a solid basis for success.

Making Sense of Standards

Know standards and checkpoints.

What do I want students to get?

How does it look when they get it?
(assessment/rubric)

What activities—performance tasks—will support students getting knowledge/skills?

Recognize which standards/checkpoints an activity supports.

Create/recognize activities which support standards and checkpoints.

Listen

Support in other content areas.✳

Joint activities with other classes ✳

How will I modify?
Flexibility with time/activities

When designing curriculum, it is essential that you know the standards in as many subjects as possible, so that you can tap into related content areas. As you explore a curriculum idea and consider the skills and concepts involved in that activity, be open to discovering what standards and checkpoints for other disciplines might be involved. This way you can judge the richness and value of each activity you consider.

26

You will want to find inventive, interesting ways of implementing the curriculum in your classroom. There are many different approaches to this challenge, including multi-disciplinary activities, process-oriented and problem-based instruction, and hands-on learning. The following ideas are just a few of the many creative teaching techniques being used by successful teachers.

MATH+WRITING = CREATIVE WAY TO REALLY LEARN MATHEMATICS

In their efforts to break out of the traditional chalk-talk format, mathematics teachers have found it useful to incorporate other disciplines, particularly those that require different forms of thinking and different types of assessment, into their classroom activities. Research shows that excessive emphasis on drill-and-skill teaching strategies and the accompanying methods of assessment keeps students functioning at the lower levels of Bloom's Taxonomy, and prevents them from acquiring higher-order thinking skills. Writing-to-learn has been implemented with great success in mathematics instruction, as it is not merely an expansion of the traditional curriculum, but a strategy for helping students to really assimilate the essential content of that curriculum.

In the act of writing, students learn to explain the process of problem solving, and demonstrate comprehension of abstract concepts by paraphrasing ideas and by devising their own examples. Through research summaries, technical reports, explanations for the layperson, illustrations, flow charts, and skits, students learn how to present or market their mathematical ideas, and how to model abstract concepts for others. They observe that creativity is an integral aspect of the problem-solving process. They also learn from actual practice that their unique personal talents, as well as material gleaned from other content areas, can enrich their understanding of mathematics.

College-bound students and career-track students can practice expository and argumentative writing, which are key components of a writing-to-learn mathematics program. Students also hone their technical writing skills as they describe algorithms and outline logical arguments. The need for precision in technical writing can be brought into focus by having students prepare flow charts for skills as ordinary as sharpening a pencil or making a peanut butter sandwich.

One of the most important things about writing-to-learn assignments is that they provide documentation of the students' comprehension of mathematical concepts and their attitudes toward mathematical endeavors. Research projects, models, and diagrams are performance assessments that provide meaningful data about each student's progress. Such products facilitate longitudinal assessment of the learner's growth in problem-solving and communication skills.

SHORT WRITES

The deficiencies of the quarterly tests that many school districts mandate, and the anxiety that springs from the frenzied cramming and instructional interruptions associated with this testing, have convinced experienced teachers to use short writing assignments consistently and informally as a means of mathematics assessment. You can write a series of brief open-ended questions correlated with the objectives of your department's mathematics curricula. These writing prompts can be keyed to significant sections of the textbook for each course. Combining review of prerequisite concepts with the application of new vocabulary words, theorems, and/or algorithms, these short writes can be a source of creativity, humor, imagination, and real-life applications. They can be used as quizzes, warm-up exercises, and short essay addenda to conventional homework assignments. Such open-ended questions represent valuable supplements to the drill-and-skill exercises so typical of mathematics instruction.

In addition to short writes, you might want to supplement or replace each standardized chapter test with a unit project in which the students can creatively employ their writing, communication, and artistic skills to probe the nuances of a mathematical theme from the given chapter. Employing their unique talents and pursuing their own plans, subject to your approval, gives students a feeling of autonomy and confidence. As they write, draw, videotape, and construct models, your students can become authors of genuine mathematical documents, and provide you, the teacher, with a rich source of in-depth, process-oriented assessments.

WRITING-TO-LEARN MATH PROJECTS

When it comes to designing activities that combine math and writing, the possibilities are endless. One experienced math teacher shared some of her favorite activities, which may give you some ideas.

"I ask my algebra students to demonstrate their understanding of the Zero Product Property method of solving quadratic equations by having them assume the role of an algebraic air traffic controller. Their mission is to talk a student pilot through the steps of a successful landing.

"In my geometry class, I have each student assume the role of a particular geometric shape and compare his/her personal characteristics to those of other shapes. I have received postcards from the edge of the coordinate plane, and have chuckled over diary entries from Tracy Trapezoid, an insecure adolescent quadrilateral who feels that she simply doesn't measure up to the angular accomplishments of her 'perfect' parallelogram siblings.

"In one of my favorite projects, 'Conversing with the Giants,' we explore the lives of the great mathematicians. This unit requires students to integrate a variety of disciplines, including social studies and history, through a creative writing assignment and a problem-solving approach."

SCIENTIFIC LITERACY: STUDENTS AS PRACTITIONERS

Science education, like mathematics instruction, has traditionally emphasized the acquisition of content information. Unfortunately, this approach often results in the teacher racing across the breadth of the field, rather than digging thoughtfully into important scientific concepts. Research shows that the most effective teaching strategies are those that engage the students not simply as learners of science, but as practitioners. Scientific literacy means using scientific and technological information and processes to define and solve real-life problems.

 Design projects, presentations, and lab activities with the goal not only of preparing your students to meet district standards, but of bringing the scientific concepts to life. Veteran science teachers have identified three essential skills that they want their students to be capable of:

1. Demonstrating their knowledge of the basic concepts and vocabulary of physical science and technology.

2. Forming hypotheses, designing procedures to test those hypotheses through collection and analysis of data, and drawing conclusions based on their own experimentation.

3. Solving problems using critical thinking skills, scientific and technological tools, and information.

Although, as a teacher, you may occasionally assume the traditional role of dispenser of information, your primary responsibilities are to design problems appropriate to the students' level of maturity, to guide students in their investigations, to coach them in the development of needed skills, and to assess their progress toward the achievement of your stated goals. Experienced teachers suggest the following three types of activity as successful models:

1. Students work in small groups to solve problems and create products, reports, or presentations. Each group is expected to analyze the assigned problem in terms of what they already know and what they need to know. The students develop a strategy for finding necessary information (via textbooks, reference books, CD ROMs, or the Internet), plan their project, and present their learning.

2. Students engage in original scientific research, such as collection and analysis of water or air samples. Data collected can be saved and used as base-line information for year-to-year studies.

3. Students apply scientific theory in the creation of technological products or models, and test and redesign those products or models to achieve the desired results.

For students to develop a true understanding of the role of science in society, science should not be taught in isolation, but in relationship to the many spheres of human experience that both affect and are affected by it, including ethics, culture, law, economics, and politics. When designing a problem or activity, try to enrich the science learning with information and perspectives from as many related areas as you can. This process often leads to an increased level of student engagement as they discover the numerous ways in which the material applies to their lives.

Hands-on Science

EFFECTS OF POLLUTION ON AN ECOSYSTEM

Here are some examples of the type of questions that can engage students in active research and analytic thought, and involve them in a wide variety of learning activities:

—How do sediments, nutrients, and eutrophication help and harm an ecosystem?
—How can sewage help and harm an ecosystem?
—How can toxic chemicals pollute the ground water?
—Is there any clean air anywhere?
—What is acid rain and what damage is it doing to the ecosystem?
—How can deforestation cause the greenhouse effect?
—How can the globe warm and what will happen when it does?
—How can atmospheric shields be damaged and why should we care?
—Who really does the polluting and who really pays for it?

CONNECTING THE CLASSROOM TO THE REAL WORLD

There is no more powerful reward than seeing your students make meaningful connections between school learning and their real life experience. But bringing the real world into the classroom is no easy task. It means something different for each group of students and involves continual experimentation on the part of the teacher.

One successful teaching method is a multi-skill program based on sets of written directions that students follow, either individually or in groups. These directions lead them through a series of reading, writing, math, science, and prevocational activities, which end in a tangible product that is useful or interesting to the students.

"On a typical day, my sixth grade students filter into the classroom at 10:30 in the morning and turn in their homework. They get their instructions from the project box in the back of the room, and pick up where they left off in the previous class.

"Michael and Tanya are two such sixth grade students. They are building a clock out of cardboard and a $2.00 clock mechanism. So far they have read five pages of instructions. They have figured out that there are 360 degrees in a circle and that there are 30 degrees between each of the numbers on a circular clock face. Using that information, a compass, a protractor, and numerous other math skills, they've completed a paper diagram of the clock and marked the locations of the clock numerals. Next, as instructed, they will ask for a calculator to figure out the sine and cosine of the various angles.

"Then it's off to the computer where they'll open a spread sheet program. They'll enter sine and cosine data, along with the formulas to find the X and Y coordinates of the clock numerals (all of which they figured out earlier). Once the data has been entered, they'll print out their spread sheet, open a Computer Assisted Design (CAD) program, and use the spread sheet data to make and print out a paper clock face. Later on, they will make paper templates, using Cartesian coordinates, with which they'll construct the cardboard clock base. But before that happens, the bell rings, the sixth graders leave, and my eighth graders come in. They are making airplane wings for 17.5 inch Styrofoam gliders.

"The method has worked so well that the students sometimes don't even recognize these projects as part of their school learning. Carmen, one of my students, pointed this out to me last year after she had completed a unit on making a jewelry box for her mother. Over the course of the unit she had learned and applied ruler skills to make a Cartesian coordinate grid; decimal and fraction skills to plot points on the grid; protractor and compass skills to make circles, angles, and arcs; and measurement skills to find cylindrical dowel rods and drill bits of differing diameters. At the end of one class she noticed a mathematics textbook on my desk and asked, 'Do you teach math in this class too?'"

CLASSROOM QUILTS: EXPLORING FAMILY, CULTURE, AND HISTORY

In any classroom, but particularly a multicultural classroom, a quilting project can be a wonderful vehicle for students to exchange information about themselves and their families. Quilting and other activities involving textiles are prevalent in most cultures and tap into a rich source of social and family history. In addition to the obvious focus on design, measurement, and craft skills, a quilting project can be taken in countless directions, depending on the age of the students and the instructional goals of the teacher. Research, written accounts, oral history presentations, and creative writing projects are just a few possibilities.

In the course of the project each student creates a miniature quilt comprised of four six-inch squares of fabric, at least one of which came from that student's family. The pieces of fabric might be taken from the garments of family members who are to be remembered in some way. They may also come from old pieces of clothes or baby blankets used by the students themselves. Other articles such as barrettes, buttons, pins, and interesting trinkets can be sewn into the fabric, or placed where the fabric is tacked. When the class is ready to assemble the quilt, the individual pieces—miniature quilts—can be loosely sewn together with large stitches, or taped side by side on the wall; so that these individual pieces can be easily returned to their owners. When it is complete, the quilt, which should include a piece from each student, can be displayed in the classroom or any other appropriate place in the school.

In preparation for the project, have students practice measuring and cutting six-inch squares from sheets of paper. They can draw designs and patterns on these squares and try out different arrangements. Younger students do not have to cut the actual fabric squares that go into their quilts, but should be encouraged to help with the sewing, which they can practice prior to the activity. The actual assemblage of the quilt can be a complicated process, so do not be shy about soliciting help from the students' families. Parents and grandparents who are not working are often happy to be engaged in a major class project. On the day of the activity, ask adults working with the students to reinforce any areas that the children miss. You should expect the finished products to look somewhat crude, reflecting the hands-on participation of the children. Do not strive for perfection; try to make the project as relaxed and enjoyable as possible.

TEACHING THE WRITING PROCESS

A good writing program can help students reflect on their surroundings, values, ideas, and experiences, while they develop the skills and confidence necessary to express themselves effectively on paper. There are many good ways to teach writing. Ultimately, you will arrive at the formula that works best for you and your students through experimentation and creative adaptation. We recommend an approach that is based on a four-step writing process: PREWRITING-CREATION-REVISION-PUBLICATION. Students can apply this process on every level, from the crafting of a paragraph to the creation of an essay, report, work of fiction, or piece of poetry. The publication phase can take any number of forms, from sharing the work in class or placing it in a portfolio, to desktop publishing individual pieces, or producing a bound collection of student writing.

Sample assignment: The "how to" essay

When you are teaching the writing process, you may want to start out with a relatively structured assignment, such as a five-paragraph essay. The clarity of this structure gives students a chance to focus on the process and develop their individual styles. One successful model is the instructional essay, which explains how to do something in three steps or stages.

Begin by having students read an example of an instructional essay that deals with a topic relevant to their experience, such as "How to Behave at a Rock Concert" or "How to Explain a Poor Report Card to Your Parents." Students brainstorm a list of possible topics, choose one with which they feel comfortable, and list the three to five steps they intend to demonstrate.

Tell students to ignore the introductory paragraph at this point and concentrate on creating, revising, and developing each of the body paragraphs. In the PREWRITING phase for the first body paragraph, ask the class, "If a person were to demonstrate only the first step in front of the class, what questions would you as the audience want to have answered?" Invariably, the students will arrive at these four questions:

1. What step is being demonstrated?

2. Why is it important?

3. How is the step completed? Are there dangers to avoid or shortcuts to take?

4. What will happen if the step is completed incorrectly?

In the CREATION phase of each of the body paragraphs, students use these questions to develop a rough draft. This is where the individual skills, motivations, and experiences of the students come into play. The biggest challenge for the students is learning to explain a process that comes naturally to them to a faceless audience that may not automatically understand.

This underscores the importance of the REVISION phase and the role of the peer editor. The strengths and flaws of the rough draft are easier to discern with the help of a fresh set of eyes. (It is important that you observe these first editing experiences closely, ready to act as "the court of last resort" when disputes arise.) Each body paragraph should be submitted separately for peer editing, and the partners should use an editing rubric like the following, in order to give and receive concrete revision ideas:

	4	3	2	1
Organization				
Focus				
Depth of Detail				
Fluency and Style				
Mechanics				
Impact				

Be careful to provide students with precise definitions of the numeric valuations for each category. The following are possible valuations for Depth of Detail:

4 = Author's detail brings the step to life. He/she is an authority.
3 = Author's detail clearly illustrates the step.
2 = One or more details are lacking, or detail is consistent but poorly ordered.
1 = Explanation of the step is unrelated, vague, or absent.

The next day the authors take action on the three main suggestions made by their peer editors. This process is repeated until all the body paragraphs have been revised once. At this point, students begin the prewriting phase for the introductory paragraph. The list that they come up with for this phase will look something like this:

1. What is the process?

2. Why and when would I use it?

3. What will I need?

4. What will happen?

The beauty of the prewriting approach is that it tests students' ability to relate to an audience, write in strong detail, and write from the role of an expert. It has a healthy effect on the tone of the writing and gives students a framework in which they can experiment with humor and imaginative description. The same steps are followed for the concluding paragraph, and when that work is complete, the whole essay is submitted for a final peer-editing session. This time, an assessment scale is provided that explains how the final essay will be evaluated by the teacher.

DARE TO SHARE

Seize every opportunity to engage your students in individual and group projects that will be exhibited publicly at some point. This makes the learning real. There is a tangible goal, and it's also more fun. Here are a few ideas:

1. Finish off a unit on poetry with a student poetry reading.

2. Invite other classes in to see an exhibition of your students' work.

3. Have students choose a topic to take a stand on. Engage them in research and help them develop position-taking skills. They can present and defend their theses before a board of their peers, or you can stage a debate and invite other teachers and students in to judge.

4. Following a unit on drama, have your students write plays and work together to develop them. Allow the class to choose the play or plays they want to produce and perform for other classes. Reserve the auditorium, rehearse the play(s), and put on a program.

5. Give the students a choice of books—biographies, novels, non-fiction—related to class work. Have them meet periodically in pairs or groups and work on interactive multimedia presentations to share their books with the class.

6. After a writing unit, have students lay their work out on their desks along with comment sheets. Students can then walk around the room, reading each other's work and writing down comments and personal reactions. The entire activity should be silent, museum-style.

If you take the leap of faith and allow yourself to believe that your students will rise to the occasion when challenged before the spotlight, they will. But it is up to you to create the occasions.

 34

≫ Assessment: an ongoing dialogue with your students

The most effective teachers are those who have their long-term goals firmly in mind and always have a clear sense of where their students are in relation to those goals. Assessments, in all of their variety, are tools that you can use on a regular basis to keep your teaching in step with your objectives. Do not think of assessment as a culminating and defining moment that takes place at the end of the semester or school year. Preparing students to succeed on the standardized tests is an important part of your job, but research shows that for students to gain mastery of a concept or idea, they have to be able to recognize and apply that idea in a variety of contexts. This means that throughout the school year, you need to supplement standardized testing formats with other assessment methods that give students the opportunity to fully develop and demonstrate their understanding of the "big ideas" set forth in the district standards. Students need the stimulation and challenge of processing information on many different levels, including knowledge, comprehension, application, analysis, synthesis, and evaluation. Providing your students with opportunities to apply concepts and information in a variety of formats will reinforce their knowledge and make your classroom much more lively.

There are many different forms of assessment, from simple observation, performance tasks, portfolios, and student self-assessment, to traditional tests. All sorts of student activities, including research projects, content-area journals, student-produced newsletters, creative writing assignments, small-group work, skits, educational games, oral presentations, and hands-on projects of every shape and form, are used by experienced teachers not only as instructional tools, but as assessment tools. There are as many different ways to assess your students as there are ways to teach them.

PORTFOLIOS

If you model and encourage joyful, creative engagement with the course material, then you will soon collect a wide array of interesting work from your students. In addition, you will be able to discern a process of evolution in their skill levels. The vital question becomes how best to organize these products longitudinally, in order to assess areas of weakness and to celebrate students' progress. Many teachers have found that portfolios are a useful and productive way to organize student work.

A portfolio is a folder in which the learner stores a variety of work in various stages of completion. The portfolio folder should contain many pieces, not merely polished works, and from this folder the student selects pieces to edit and polish for sharing with others. These polished pieces, as well as the collection of works in progress, document each student's range and ability as a communicator of content-specific concepts. Veteran teachers recommend a two-tier system of working portfolio and showcase portfolio. In preparing the showcase portfolio pieces each quarter, the students work with peer editors and each student selects a favorite piece from the working portfolio to expand and reshape as an example of his/her best efforts in communicating the content material, which can be anything from mathematics to language arts. Ideally, the showcase portfolio also includes a reflective essay about why particular pieces were selected.

Consulting with peers in the selection of possibilities for the showcase portfolio causes students to look more closely at their writing and ask more questions about strategies for improving their work. Teachers have found that having students keep both working and showcase portfolios fosters metacognition, encourages collaboration with peers, and facilitates authentic longitudinal assessment.

SELF-ASSESSMENT

It is critical that students assume responsibility for their own learning. One effective way to promote this is to involve students in setting goals for the class, and have them assess their progress towards achieving these goals. It can be helpful to meet regularly with individual students to evaluate their learning and refocus their goals. If your students keep portfolios, you might have them add a narrative description to each piece they save, explaining how this particular assignment meets or exceeds the goal that was set. There are many different ways in which self-assessment can become an integral part of student learning.

DESIGNING TESTS

The first thing to ask yourself when you design a test is what your objectives are. What do you want to know? What do you want your students to know? Remember that assessment should not be a "gotcha" proposition. An effective teacher acts as a coach, not an adversary. Tell students ahead of time exactly what kind of test you are giving and what it will cover. Giving a practice test and showing them how it will be evaluated is a good way to prepare them. A test should cover only the material that you have read or discussed with your class. The length and form of the test and the depth of the questions will depend on what you are trying to assess. If you simply want to make sure your students have read a particular story, a few multiple choice questions should be adequate. But if you are testing for comprehension of a larger scope of material, or if you want to see how your students are managing a new skill, your questions or problems will have to be of greater depth and variety. Remember that a well-designed test is not only a diagnostic or an evaluative instrument, it is a teaching device.

Design your tests carefully and creatively. Take the exam yourself. How long did it take you to complete it? Did it test what you wanted it to test? Did it seem fair? Did you teach and review the work adequately? Decide whether or not you will offer a substitute test or project for those who fail the exam.

STANDARDIZED TESTS

Standardized tests are a fact of life, and it is important that you prepare your students to approach them with confidence. Most standardized tests are given at the end of the quarter, semester, or school year. Prior to the time of testing you should make note of the format that will be used—such as essay, fill in the blank, or multiple choice—and find or create materials that will familiarize your students with the test format. Obtain, if possible, a test given to your grade level the previous year. Look at the skills tested and ask yourself the following questions:

1. How is the test administered to the students? If orally, you will need to reinforce listening skills. If silently, you will need to reinforce reading skills.

2. What is the test asking the student to do?

3. What kind of distracters are put in the test?

4. Most importantly, has your curriculum really prepared your students for this test?

When gearing up for standardized tests, stress their importance but make an effort to reduce student anxiety. Practice will help your students, and they will feel more comfortable with the whole experience if they know what to expect.

A LANGUAGE ARTS UNIT INCORPORATING SELF-ASSESSMENT

Giving your students a chance to really evaluate their own work can also give you, the teacher, a deeper understanding of what your students have learned. It becomes very clear whether or not they have grasped a concept when they describe how they accomplished each part of the assignment. In this unit students write stories focusing on some specific writing techniques. The student goal is to learn and practice the following strategies:

1. Use your own experience as a starting place.
2. "Show," rather than "tell" in your writing.
3. Use realistic dialogue.
4. Revise your work.
5. Edit carefully to be sure that there are no spelling or grammar mistakes.
6. Take a risk; try something different.

You should spend several weeks exploring these strategies. Read good examples of each technique from a variety of authors. Have students practice the techniques in their own stories and share their ideas with each other. At the end of the unit, have students take their finished stories and evaluate themselves. Ask them to think critically about their writing and rank their success in meeting each of the goals on a scale from one to five. A perfect score of five means the student did his/her personal best and went "above and beyond." A three means that the individual accomplished the goal to his/her satisfaction, and a one means that the goal was not accomplished. After some discussion and a little practice, students really handle this well. Because the justification is such an important part of the learning process, you should leave your students plenty of time to fill out their evaluation sheets thoughtfully. The self-evaluation sheet for this unit looks like this:

Rank yourself from one to five on each of the following components. Describe your rationale in detail.

1. Is this story based on personal experience? Describe.
2. Give examples of how you used the concept of "showing, not telling" in your story.
3. Give examples of how you used realistic dialogue in your story.
4. What process did you use to revise your story?
5. What process did you use to edit your work?
6. How did you take a risk with this story?

Look carefully at your students' self-evaluations when you grade their work, and give points for each component, just as your students did. If your assessments occasionally differ drastically from the valuations students gave themselves, set up individual conferences with those students. In most cases, discrepancies result from students undervaluing, rather than overvaluing their work. This is a very useful assessment tool, as it gives students much more information than simple letter grades do. It also reveals which areas you need to reteach and helps you identify problems that need to be addressed with individual students.

CLASS PARTICIPATION ASSESSMENT

Name _____ Quarter _____

Your class participation is an important part of this course. You will assess yourself and your teacher will also assess you. This gives you an opportunity to reflect upon your own performance and attitude. You will rank yourself on a scale of 5-10 in each of the following areas listed in the chart. You should consider your overall participation as well as your improvement (if any) during the quarter.

Key to rankings:
5 = *Ouch!*—did not exhibit the quality at all.
6 = *Very Weak*—needs great improvement in this area.
7 = *Fair*—occasionally exhibits quality but not on a consistent basis.
8 = *O.K.*—exhibits quality a good deal of the time.
9 = *Good*—exhibits quality almost all of the time.
10 = *Outstanding*—an area of excellence and source of pride for you.

Quality	5	6	7	8	9	10
Behavior —Are you respectful of teachers and peers? Do you avoid unnecessary talking? Do you listen to others? In lab, do you follow instructions and maintain safety standards?						
Preparation—Do you complete your homework and turn it in on time? Do you bring your notebook and book to class? Do you think about the ideas and get help when you don't understand?						
Effort—Do you do your best work? Do you analyze your mistakes, learn from them, and do better the next time? Is your work of high quality—neat and thorough? Are you on time to class?						
Attitude—Do you volunteer to answer questions? Are you cooperative and enthusiastic about class activities? Do you take a leadership role in your groups? Do you avoid whining and complaining?						
Focus—Do you pay attention for the whole period? Do you take good notes and ask questions? Do you avoid packing up your materials before the bell rings?						

Student Total_____   Teacher Total_____

Comments:_____   Comments: _____

DEALING WITH "SENIOR SLACK"

Senior slack is a uniquely second semester phenomenon that is a great challenge to educators. Veteran teachers have found that the most effective way to deal with it is to confront it head-on. Seniors are no longer motivated by grades, but they do care deeply about what others think of their work. Instead of a final exam, try end-of-the-year projects (for example, in a biology class, the projects may be on some aspect of human health), which they can present at an exhibition night at the end of the year, and to which parents and the community can be invited. The projects can involve extensive research and all sorts of creative applications.

To grade these projects, it is helpful to use rubrics (such as the sample on the facing page). Give the students the rubrics in advance, and their projects will be much better as a result of knowing exactly what is expected of them. To develop a rubric, you must decide on the criteria that you want to evaluate, and how much weight you want to give to each of the criteria. Then you must decide on the characteristics that will fit each of the possible grades or point values. Rubrics are useful in assessing all sorts of projects that defy easy evaluation, and are especially useful with seniors, since it is precisely these more complex projects and presentations that seem to capture the special energy and momentum of the graduating class.

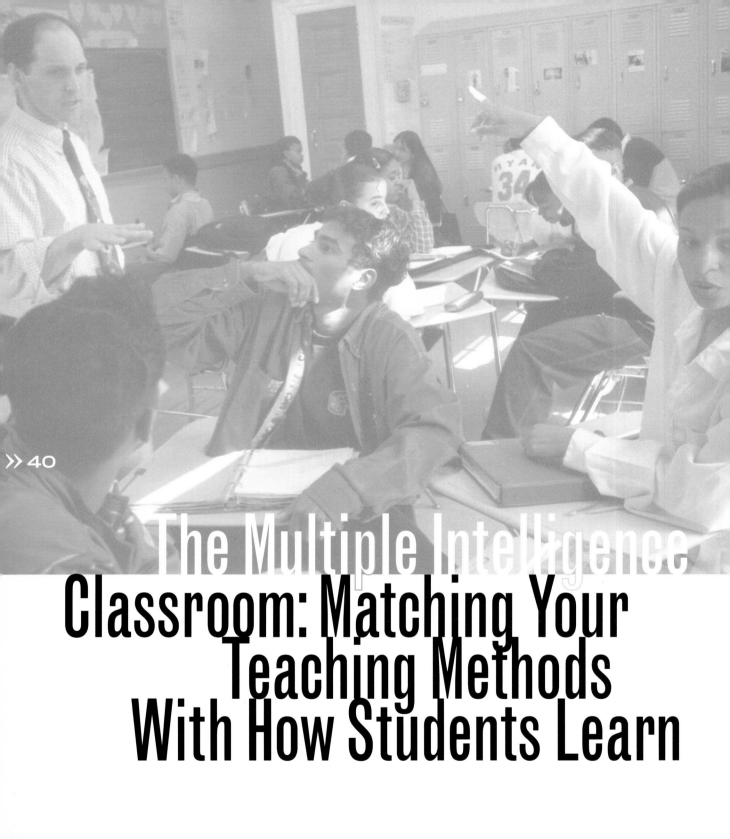

The Multiple Intelligence Classroom: Matching Your Teaching Methods With How Students Learn

I f you subscribe to the theory that all students can learn, then it is important for you, as an educator, to equip yourself with as many strategies as possible to reach those students who do not seem to learn well from the more traditional teaching methods. Many students are frustrated by their lack of success in the school environment, which measures primarily reading and mathematics skills. They may fall into a routine of convincing themselves and their teachers that they cannot succeed no matter what they do, as they have been led to believe that they are intellectually inferior to their classmates who score higher on tests. In fact, these students could be very successful in careers that require other aptitudes, such as mechanics, art, music, design, and a whole range of professions that focus on interpersonal skills. By recognizing and building on your students' strengths, you can help them develop the tools they need to succeed.

» Gardner's theory of multiple intelligences

"We must organize teaching around students' learning."
—Linda Darling-Hammond

Howard Gardner, a professor at Harvard's Graduate School of Education, theorizes that people are intelligent in different ways. This is a relatively new way of looking at intelligence, as schools have traditionally measured it by IQ scores. According to Gardner's theory, each person is born with a full range of capacities and aptitudes, though some are naturally stronger, and some naturally weaker in each individual. These differences do not indicate that one person is more or less intelligent than the next, but simply that each one learns, thinks, processes, and produces differently.

A person's preference for a particular intelligence greatly influences how that person learns. For example, a verbal learner learns by using words, while a kinesthetic learner learns and expresses him/herself best through physical movement. Your goal should be to recognize and take advantage of the natural learning styles of all of your students, while helping them to improve the skills that are weaker. The more skillful you become at working with multiple intelligences, the more your students will learn, and the more lively and engaging your classroom will be.

Research has shown that many discipline "problems" can also be understood and dealt with by applying the theory of multiple intelligences. What teachers used to think of as "petty annoyances" can tell you a great deal about a student's intelligence profile. Not all students will be quiet when you request it, and if they are, they may not all be giving you their full attention. Some students have difficulty sitting still even for short periods of time. Others tap their feet or pencils without even realizing they are doing it, or that it is disturbing to other students. Some are constantly daydreaming. Some are extremely quiet and do not participate in class. Others are always whispering to their neighbors. If you think of these behaviors not simply as discipline problems, but as learning challenges, you can help your students channel their natural tendencies into productive means for learning.

Below we have outlined Gardner's different types of intelligence, and for each type, a variety of classroom activities through which students can demonstrate their learning. Many of the activities overlap, as there are certain elements that apply to more than one type of intelligence.

VERBAL/LINGUISTIC INTELLIGENCE

The most important skill taught in school is the ability to use language for effective communication. Language skills include reading, writing, listening, speaking, and making connections. This intelligence goes beyond simple verbal and grammatical tasks; it is the basis for creating stories, using metaphors and similes, symbolic thinking, and conceptual patterning. Our experience has demonstrated that verbal intelligence can be brought out through the use of humor, jokes, puns, plays on words, and other creative language manipulations.

Students who are strong in this type of intelligence learn best by repeating, saying out loud, hearing, and seeing words, but rely on a variety of different learning techniques. Many students learn better from hearing words spoken orally than they do from silent reading, and you may find that these students like to read out loud to themselves, which can be disruptive to the class. They may appear rude and disinterested in class when their eyes wander from the written text, but in fact they could just be trying to shut out distractions and absorb the material aurally. Rather than viewing this as a discipline problem, try to find ways to accommodate students who learn best aurally.

A student with highly developed verbal/linguistic intelligence and an active imagination may have trouble engaging in subject matter that does not tap into this natural proclivity, and may even do poorly in school as a result of disinterest. Fortunately, most subject areas can be approached through a verbal route and this type of student should be encouraged to apply his/her verbal creativity in as many areas as possible. Personal attention can be very encouraging to these students and you may want to display their work in class, or ask them to read aloud to the class. At the same time, be aware that because they have heightened language sensibilities, all forms of non-constructive verbal criticism such as sarcasm, negative comments, and humiliation can completely turn them off to learning.

Classroom activities that tap into this type of intelligence include:
* Writing a journal.
* Creating a real or imagined correspondence between historical or contemporary characters.
* Composing scripts that depict historical events.
* Writing newspapers of a different time period, complete with then-current events, fashion, entertainment, and feature items.
* Rewriting difficult information in a simpler form for younger students.
* Interviewing a famous person with knowledge of a topic, or whose accomplishments are admired.

* Inviting a guest speaker and planning appropriate questions.
* Reading poetry or writing poetry, stories, ideas, or thoughts.
* Creating analogies to explain concepts.
* Designing bulletin boards.
* Using recording devices.
* Doing dramatic readings.

MUSICAL/RHYTHMIC INTELLIGENCE

Students who are strong in this type of intelligence learn most readily through rhythm, melody, and music. They like to sing, hum, listen to music, and/or play instruments. They are good at picking up sounds, remembering melodies, noticing rhythms, and keeping time, and can easily memorize words that have been set to music.

These students often prefer to tell or hear information aloud rather than read silently. Soft music in the background helps them focus and concentrate on their work. They may have trouble concentrating on a lesson if they cannot find a way to link the subject to music. They often use mnemonic devices and put words to melodies to help them memorize facts, rules, and procedures. It can help these students focus if you incorporate popular songs from the places and time periods being studied in class. They should be encouraged to make up rhymes and catchy rhythmic phrases that contain the material they need to study. They may enjoy teaching rhythmic patterns, vocal sounds, and musical tones to others; composing music; and choreographing dances.

Activities that bring this intelligence out in students and can help them prove mastery of content include:
* Writing an original song, rap, jingle, or cheer.
* Playing instruments.
* Composing music that conveys the theme or mood of the lesson.
* Researching, comparing, and contrasting music of different cultures or time periods.
* Identifying rhythmic patterns in music or poetry.
* Creating a rhythmic way to remember information.
* Performing a rap or song that summarizes information.

LOGICAL/MATHEMATICAL INTELLIGENCE

The subjects most often associated with logical/mathematical intelligence are math and science; however, the skills involved can be applied to almost any content area. These skills include the capacities for inductive and deductive reasoning, understanding and applying abstract concepts, and critical thinking.

Students with a high level of this type of intelligence like to develop strategies, perform experiments, reason things out, work with numbers, ask questions, and explore patterns and relationships. They learn best by categorizing or classifying new information, and working with abstract patterns. They work well with symbols and formulas, are able to solve complex problems, logic games, and puzzles, and are good at deciphering codes. They are highly methodical and will carefully examine their past experiences when determining what their next move will be. They work well with problem-solving tools such as computers and calculators. Their thought processes are mostly sequential, and they can therefore find their own mistakes when given an explanation. They may question assignments or become immobilized if directions are too open-ended, but at the same time these learners often want to solve problems in their own way and might argue with a teacher who cannot accept alternative methods. They will challenge any concept that does not make sense immediately according to their own ordered universe. These students are easily bored by repetitive activities and need to be engaged in the challenge of problem solving in order to connect to their work.

Activities that take advantage of this type of intelligence and allow students to demonstrate their understanding include:
* Creating trivia games that others can play.
* Developing crossword and other puzzles for classmates to solve.
* Constructing a time line and filling in details.
* Writing how-to books.
* Investigating authentic problems and developing possible solutions.
* Mapping a location.
* Diagramming procedures.
* Creating a "web" organizer or Venn diagram to organize information to present to others.
* Using pattern blocks, unifix cubes, Legos, and other math manipulatives to demonstrate concepts.
* Playing calculator games.
* Conducting research and laboratory experiments.
* Categorizing facts and information.
* Composing analogies.

VISUAL/SPATIAL INTELLIGENCE

People who demonstrate visual/spatial intelligence tend to focus on the visual arts or the use of objects in their learning. They have acute perception of form, shape, depth, color, and texture, and are able to form clear images in their minds. They tend to have active imaginations and are adept at expressing themselves through original drawings, paintings, sculptures, design patterns, and color schemes.

These students respond well to visual aids such as overhead projectors, maps, posters, photographs, and videos. They may find it difficult to read long passages that are not accompanied by illustrations, to write, or to communicate in general with words. Most younger elementary students enjoy expressing themselves through this aptitude.

Activities that give students a chance to display their knowledge through visual/spatial intelligence include:
* Drawing or painting a picture, poster, chart, or sketch representing what they have learned.
* Making a three-dimensional model such as a physical map.
* Creating colorful designs, shapes, and patterns to illustrate a scene from nature or history.

* Imagining and visualizing how literary or historic figures might
    have changed events.
* Taking photographs or using a video camera to create a pictorial report.
* Constructing props and costumes to dramatize an event.
* Creating Venn diagrams or concept maps to explain information to others.
* Developing color-coding systems to categorize information.
* Building a shadow box or diorama display.

BODY/KINESTHETIC INTELLIGENCE

The person whose strength lies in body/kinesthetic intelligence feels a compulsion to bridge the gap between mind and body. This type of student learns through touching, physical movement, manipulating concrete objects, and interacting with his/her environment. Activities that tap into this type of intelligence include dancing, role playing, drama, gesticulations, physical exercise, sports, mime, and martial arts.

These students feel most comfortable in a classroom environment where they have the freedom to stand, stretch, and move at regular intervals. They may invent reasons to get up from their desks, as they have a real physiological need to move. If they are not permitted to move when they need to, they can become bored, distracted, anxious, and disruptive. Cooperative learning, jigsaw activities in which each member of a group is responsible for teaching the others one part of the whole story, and role playing are formats that these students respond well to. In the younger grades, numerous games and activities that incorporate movement are popular and successful. Students can learn the letters of the alphabet by shaping their bodies like those letters. They can also trace new letters in a box of sand or on sandpaper.

Students who are strong in this type of intelligence can demonstrate their mastery of content through:
* Dramatizing a literary or historical event.
* Role playing.
* Creating a dance or movement that tells a story.
* Going on field trips to appropriate sites.
* Participating in learning centers.
* Learning outdoors.
* Acting out vocabulary words or a sequence of events.
* Constructing projects and making diagrams, models, or replicas of
    systems or procedures.
* Building puppets and putting on a show related to content.
* Pantomiming a sequence.
* Playing charades.

INTERPERSONAL INTELLIGENCE

Interpersonal intelligence is displayed primarily through communication, positive interaction, and the formation of positive personal relationships. It also entails the ability to see situations from various perspectives and the desire to motivate others towards a common goal. Individuals with highly developed interpersonal intelligence are team players and possess strong leadership qualities.

As learners, they have a preference for solving problems by discussing them first in a group and coming up with a common solution. They are skilled at understanding people, organizing, collaborating, communicating, and mediating conflicts. Their true concern for others can lead them to ignore their own needs, but you can help them focus on their learning by creating opportunities for them to be helpful to others while developing their skills. These students enjoy cooperative learning, one-on-one peer tutoring, and exercises that ask them to identify with a character or figure they are studying.

Students with a high level of interpersonal intelligence can demonstrate their knowledge through:

* Participating in jigsaw activities, where each person in a group is responsible for specific tasks.
* Working on interactive computer software, e-mail, and the Internet.
* Joining any group project.
* Sharing cooperative learning strategies.
* Identifying with figures in art or literature.
* Studying or creating oral histories.
* Interviewing or creating imaginary interviews with relevant people (real, historical, or literary).
* Constructing a family tree.
* Peer tutoring.

INTRAPERSONAL INTELLIGENCE

The essential component of this intelligence is knowledge of the self. This means being in tune with one's emotions, thought processes, attitudes, and reactions, and taking responsibility for one's choices and actions, especially for one's learning.

A student who has a high level of intrapersonal intelligence may have a strong will, control over his/her emotions, and the ability to plan in advance and set independent personal goals. The energy and focus of these learners can be a catalyst for other students, though at times their interests may take them in directions that have little relationship to class goals. These students generally prefer to work alone, but they do need a lot of one-on-one interaction, guidance, and reinforcement from their teacher. This type of student may feel uncomfortable in groups and may not voluntarily participate in class discussions, though he/she is stimulated by thought-provoking questions, and is capable of contributing a unique perspective.

These students sometimes appear excessively quiet and withdrawn and may even exhibit antisocial behavior as a result of failing to recognize the needs of others. You can help them connect in a positive way with their peers by creating opportunities for them to share their original ideas, knowledge, and research with other students.

Activities that engage and assist intrapersonal learners include:
* Writing journal entries that summarize content and any personal reactions to content.
* Completing independent assignments.
* Meeting with the teacher outside of class.
* Investigating complex problems.
* Researching topics of interest.
* Reflecting in a journal about their learning process.
* Creating personal files of topics they have studied.
* Writing first-person accounts of events.
* Personalizing a character and writing his/her "autobiography."
* Constructing a bibliography that can be used by others.
* Self-assessing projects and products to determine how to improve learning.

NATURALIST INTELLIGENCE

The person with a strong naturalist intelligence will recognize and discriminate among objects found in our natural world.

Naturalists watch and observe the environment. They appreciate and discern differences among living things, and have a keen interest in the laws and forms of nature. They enjoy going on hikes and being outdoors. Naturalists will care for the classroom pet and plants, organize and sort classroom collections of rocks, shells, leaves, insects, and other items from nature, and categorize anything.

Activities the naturalist will enjoy include:
* Going on field trips and nature walks.
* Forecasting and tracking the weather.
* Observing the sky, clouds, stars, and space.
* Hiking in natural surroundings.
* Reporting on nature videos.
* Listing attributes of objects.
* Recording changes or development over time.
* Photographing nature.
* Devising classifications.
* Sorting and categorizing items.
* Caring for plants and animals.
* Using graphic organizers.
* Reconstructing the natural setting in a historical place.
* Predicting the effects of extreme natural phenomena.

» Adapting Gardner's theory to an authentic classroom

You can help your students gain self-esteem by giving them the opportunity to demonstrate mastery of their subjects while expressing themselves through their most highly-developed intelligences. This is not to say, however, that you should gear activities only to the students' strengths. On the contrary, you should work to improve your students' skills in all areas, so that they will be prepared to undertake tasks that tap their weaker abilities as well.

In a real classroom situation, you cannot individualize instruction for each of your students. It is simply not a realistic goal. What you can do is teach in a variety of ways and regularly offer an exciting range of activities to your students. When you are planning a unit, try to incorporate various types of intelligences into the activities. A natural way to accomplish this is by teaching in an interdisciplinary format. Life is an integrated experience, and integrating subjects can make the content more meaningful to students.

Here is an example from a high school science class. The goal of the project is to analyze local water purity. Samples from various taps and nearby bodies of water are collected and sent for testing to the local Environmental Protection Agency. EPA agents and town or city officials can be interviewed. Local newspapers can become sources of information. Then results can be compared. Charts and diagrams can be developed. Models can be constructed. Students can reflect on the results and report them in a variety of ways. This problem-based assignment involves the gathering of data, hypothesizing, synthesizing, reading, writing, reporting, interpreting information, making references, and working collaboratively. The teacher has incorporated math, science, reading, and writing into this single project.

Ultimately, the most important skill you can impart to your students is the ability to solve problems. It is not enough to identify your students' stronger and weaker intelligences and teach accordingly. Rather, it is essential that you make your students aware of their own talents, learning processes, and potential. You want to prepare them to face problems with confidence; with a knowledge of which personal resources they can tap into and which new strategies they feel comfortable trying out. This self-knowledge is perhaps the best preparation you can give them for the future.

For More Information

This chapter is based on the work of Howard Gardner. If you want more information on Gardner's theory and would like to go straight to the source, check out these books:

Gardner, Howard. *Multiple Intelligences: The Theory in Practice.* New York: Basic Books, 1993.

Gardner, Howard. *Frames of Minds: The Theory of Multiple Intelligences.* New York: Basic Books, 1983.

You can contact Howard Gardner, co-director of Project Zero, a research group at the Harvard Graduate School of Education, at:

Project Zero
Harvard Graduate School of Education
321 Longfellow Hall
13 Appian Way
Cambridge, MA 02138
e-mail: info@pz.harvard.edu

Families as
Partners

Historically, teachers were focused simply on providing children with the best educational program possible. The home environment provided everything else. But today, with many single parent families and more families with two working parents, schools and teachers are major contributors not only to the child's learning, but also to his/her day-to-day care. Schools have become responsible for the physical care of children, breakfast and lunch programs, and daycare before and after school. As the role of teachers in students' lives has become more diversified, it is more important than ever that teachers develop strong partnerships with families to insure that parents and other caregivers are fully informed, truly involved, and provide as much support as possible to the educational process.

What do students' families expect from teachers and what do teachers want from families? A successful partnership requires that each partner have a concrete understanding of the other's expectations for the relationship. What students' families expect from teachers is a commitment to the highest professional standards. They also expect teachers to be responsible for the results of their instructional programs and accountable for the students' learning. But teachers need no less of a commitment from students' families. When the subject of parents or parent participation comes up, you will generally hear a long list of complaints from veteran teachers. Most of these complaints boil down to one basic theme: **THEY don't participate enough in their child's school experience.**

——THEY don't oversee the homework each night, making sure it's done and/or done properly.
__THEY don't volunteer for field trips.
——THEY don't make an appointment before coming to school to talk to the teacher.
——THEY don't sign in at the front desk before coming to the classroom.
——THEY don't make their children complete special projects.
——THEY do their child's special projects.
——THEY blame the teacher for their child's faults.
——THEY don't respond to notes sent home.
——THEY defend their child instead of backing up the teacher in disputes.

While these complaints are often well-founded, the fact is that parents and family members are rarely included in pleasant, non-threatening school experiences. Apart from impersonal group invitations to holiday assemblies and open houses, parents are generally invited to school only to get the report card, or when their child is being punished for a behavior infraction, both of which are understandably threatening experiences.

Teachers need students' families to share in the responsibility and accountability for the outcome of their children's education, but it is incumbent upon you, the teacher, to make the partnership possible. You must realize the power you wield in the parent-teacher relationship. It is up to you to open a friendly dialogue, establish firm lines of communication between home and school, and welcome parents and family members into their children's school lives.

» Presenting yourself to students' families and enlisting their support

Begin in September to reach out to students' families. Several avenues of communication should be explored as you work to establish a strong partnership. Regular written communications, parent conferences, phone calls, and open classroom activities can each play an important role in developing good rapport with students' families. The following suggestions can help you get started:

1. Be positive. Parents and other family members want the same thing you do for their children: a good education. You will win support if you let them know you expect that you and your students will have a successful, productive year. They will want to be part of the good things happening for their children.

2. Clarify expectations—yours and theirs. Introductory newsletters, bulletins, or parent/student/teacher commitment forms can all be used effectively to establish communication. Let students' families know how you will direct the learning in your classroom, and what you expect from your students. What are your goals for the class? What are your class rules and grading system? When will report cards or other forms of assessment come home? Do parents come to school for conferences? Can a telephone conference be arranged when necessary? What special activities will families be invited to attend or participate in? What can parents do if their child is having difficulty with you or your class? How can students' families support you? Try to make your written communications brief and regular, and be sure to provide an opportunity for questions, responses, and suggestions on any communication you send home.

3. Encourage students' families to take part in their child's learning. Let them know how important they are to their child's success. Help them feel welcome at school. Inform parents about their child's progress by sending corrected work home regularly. You might want to keep a folder for each student's work, which can be sent home, signed by a parent or family member after review, and returned to school.

4. Be realistic and flexible in your expectations. For some families, reasonable involvement may be limited to reading school notices, overseeing homework, and talking with their child about school. Others will have the time and inclination to become much more involved. Be ready to acknowledge all parents and family members in their efforts to support you.

5. Provide guidelines for help with homework, Include your personal ideas along with any school homework policy. Here are a few to consider:

✳ Make students responsible for understanding and completing their assignments. Homework, as you will assign it, is an extension of your classroom activities. Students will be practicing concepts and processes you have introduced and explained, or they will use ideas from your classroom as a foundation for creating something new or exploring a subject further. Make it clear that you do not expect parents or caregivers to teach or try to guess what you are asking their child to do.

✳ Let parents know that if a child forgets his/her book or does not remember how to complete an assignment, they can make this a learning experience by helping the child think through the steps or options for solving the problem. Can the child write down what he/she does not understand and ask you the next day? Can he/she call a classmate to clarify the assignment? This approach minimizes dependence on parents and helps avoid confusion for students whose parents explain subject matter in a different way than you have taught it.

✳ Explain the difference between long- and short-term assignments. Let parents know that you expect students to work within a schedule for longer assignments. If it seems appropriate, ask parents or family members to sign daily assignments and weekly progress checks on long-term homework.

✳ Ask parents and family members not to correct their child's homework. This helps to discourage an overzealous parent from taking on the assignment and relieving the child of his/her responsibility. Tell your students' families that you must see the child's independent work to know whether he/she understands the assignment. Parents and family members can help best by showing interest in the children's work, emphasizing the importance of homework, and providing a time and place to study.

✳ Invite parents' comments on your homework assignments. Do they feel the assignments are too difficult or too easy? You may want to designate an hour or two each week as telephone conference time. Encourage parents and family members not to wait for formal conferences to talk with you about their concerns.

≫ Opening the doors to your classroom

Students' families respond well to a positive invitation, and given a chance, parents and other caregivers will make an effort to participate in their child's life at school. Since they do not know you very well, they will be more comfortable if you give them a chance to visit the school in a non-threatening situation. They will recognize and appreciate the efforts of a teacher who attempts to include them. There are many different types of events and hands-on activities in which students' family members can take part. With a little initiative, you can make an academic activity into a fun and festive occasion, as well as an opportunity to share your educational philosophy and get to know your students' parents or family members. It is essential for you to be sensitive to the demands on working parents and to schedule your activities for convenient times of day or evening and give plenty of notice. Experienced teachers recommend that you send out invitations to an activity at least two weeks in advance. Include RSVP slips, and have your students bring home reminders three days before the event.

"We printed invitations on the computer and each child decorated the front with a PARTY! picture. On the day of the party, we had an adult sit inside the front door of the school to admit our visitors. They signed the visitors book and got their passes right there instead of having to go to the office.

"Our first Adventure, Math with M&M's was attended by 28 adults (in addition to our 35 students!). These parents and other adults adopted children whose parents weren't able to make it for the day. We estimated, graphed, read math literature, laughed together, and ate our bags of M&M's when we were done. The relaxed smiles on the faces of the parents signaled the success of our party.

"We continued to have adult attendance in the 20+ range for activities throughout the school year and, unexpectedly, parent attendance on field trips sky-rocketed. I also had two parents volunteer to help out in the classroom on a regular basis. One became the class librarian for my out-of-control classroom lending library, and the other became my assistant for special activities."

A variety of interesting activities can be centered around holidays and include cooking, baking, or making traditional crafts. Depending on the backgrounds and interests of the family members, you might want to try an international food, sports, or dance festival. Any of these activities can incorporate academic components such as math, science, history, social sciences, or language arts.

A more informal way to involve families is to invite individuals to join in some class lessons. Most students welcome the chance to show off for their parents by teaching them how to use a computer program or how to do an art activity. It also works well to have a parent or family member come in to demonstrate a skill or teach a special lesson. Family interviews, biographies, and research projects are other ways through which the experiences of families can be integrated into the children's educational program.

Some teachers have found that establishing a brown bag lunch policy is a good way of keeping in touch with students' families. You might consider making yourself available in the classroom during your lunch period for one day each month, so that parents or family members can drop in for a quick visit, just to see what is going on. These visits should not be thought of as conferences and should be open to anyone who shows up.

Whatever works best for you and your students, it's important that you provide families with an opportunity to participate in their children's school experience, that you give them a chance to get to know you a little bit, and that you encourage them to share in your commitment to their children's learning.

» Working with families for literacy

In a society that values literacy, perhaps nothing is more important to families and teachers than having children learn to read well and develop a lifelong love of reading. Reading aloud to children of any age has been shown to be the most effective way to foster a love of books and reading. Make every effort to get parents and families involved in reading with and to children on a regular basis as early as possible.

Suggest to students and families that they acquire library cards for the public library. Some public libraries will send representatives to the schools to talk to students about obtaining cards and making use of the library. Where it seems appropriate, encourage families to start their own personal libraries. Finally, create a classroom lending library. You may be able to get funding through your school, your district, or civic organizations. If not, you can solicit donations from the community, from businesses, or from charitable friends. To get students involved in reading, it is essential that you create an environment in which a variety of books are immediately accessible.

≫ Parent conferences

Parent conferences are generally an opportunity for teachers to learn more about their students. Parents or caregivers will trust your opinion more if you make it clear to them that you view them as the experts when it comes to understanding their child. It is also important for parents to know that the school is aware of the difficulties and challenges of parenting, and that teachers are available with information and support when needed.

One way to open positive communication with even the most difficult parents is to assure them that you value and cherish their child too. Do not put them in the position of having to take a stand against you in order to protect their child. Before you begin running down the list of what needs to be improved by that child, let the parents know some of the things you have noticed that make the child special to you and to the class as a whole. It puts you on a more empathetic footing with the parent and gets everyone on track for working together in the best interests of that child.

"Whenever I am faced with a tough conference, I spend some quiet time imagining how I would feel if I were the parent of the young person in question. Is the student bright but irresponsible? Is the student hostile or uncommunicative? Is the student truly a slow learner who will always have difficulty with this subject?"

You may decide quite accurately that the parent or family is at fault for not teaching the child responsibility or for causing the child stress. But try to remember, it is quite painful to face your own child's lack of success in school; it is even more painful to accept the fact that you might be part of the problem. So when you sit down, be prepared to offer a sympathetic ear and some words of understanding for the pain the parent or family member is experiencing, and be willing to try some of his/her suggestions. Offer your own solutions not as mandates or subtle judgements, but as helpful ideas.

It is true that families are hoping a teacher will offer a miracle. But more often than not, they recognize our humanity; in the face of true understanding, most parents are friendly, helpful, and quite reasonable. It is a good idea to ask the parents or family members if the child has had problems in other classes. Invariably, the answer will be "yes," which depersonalizes the situation and makes problem-solving more objective. If you sense an adversarial situation, your responsibility is to diffuse it and to create an environment where the primary goal—helping a young person—can be met.

In the case of high school students, it is important to have the student present for most conferences. There is not much value in conferencing with only the parent when you are dealing with a reluctant or disinterested student. You will rarely find a solution unless you include the student and listen to what he/she has to say. Ask the student for suggestions on how to help him/her become more successful. Occasionally you will find that though the student is present, the parent or family member does all of the talking, even when you turn to the student and ask a direct question. In this situation, it is helpful to tell the parent or caregiver that you are interested in his/her view, but you would really like to hear what the child has to say.

When students are not doing their work, parents will often ask you to send home lists of missing work so that they can control the completion of it. You might want to agree to this as a temporary measure, but remind the parent that your mutual goal should be to develop a

55 ≪

self-motivated and independent learner. Help parents develop a long-range plan so that they won't have to go to college with their child when he/she has graduated! Whenever possible, try to meet students' families halfway. This will diffuse their frustration and make them more open to suggestions.

Occasionally, you may find yourself dealing with an unusually intrusive parent who makes demands on your time that you feel are unreasonable. There are techniques you can learn to protect yourself, educate the parent, and keep the relationship friendly. For example, if a parent or family member asks you to call and notify him/her every time the child fails to turn in an assignment, explain that you have many other students and you simply do not have time to call parents each time a child misses an assignment. Let the parent know, however, that you appreciate how anxious he/she is to help the child become more responsible. You could give the parent or family member your home phone number and suggest that he/she call you to check in periodically (be specific about frequency). You might want to offer to send updates directly to the parents when you are preparing grades (ask that they provide you with a self-addressed, stamped envelope). Never say yes to the impossible, but do what you can to offer parents something that may be useful.

Kindergarten Conferences

It is nice to get a glimpse of your students and establish an early relationship with their families prior to the first day of school. You might want to send out letters a couple of weeks before school starts, scheduling conferences with the families, and asking them to confirm the time slots. Schedule conferences in the late afternoon or evening to alleviate conflicts for working parents. As each family comes in, you can chat with the child, briefly assess his/her knowledge and skills, and talk to the parents about your program while the child plays with blocks and puzzles. This breaks the ice, so that you and the student are not strangers on the first day. You may want to give each child a small welcome gift such as a sticker or bookmark, and let the parents know when you will be meeting with them again.

This conference time also gives you an opportunity to recruit volunteers to help out in the classroom. Although it is a significant investment of your personal time, it pays off in the long run when working with kindergartners. Remember that for many families, this is their first contact with the school. Your importance and significance to their child's education should not be minimized. Good luck and enjoy the journey!

» Encourage ongoing communication and mutual support

You will find opportunities all year long to show students' families that you value the information and support they give you. Once you have reached out to them, communicated your expectations, and understood theirs, encourage them to inform you of any situations that may cause problems for their child in school. These include the death of a pet, friend, or family member; serious illness in the family; divorce; separation; relocation; or the birth of a brother or sister. By keeping the lines of communication open—via face-to-face meetings, phone calls, home visits—you can help insure that you will be informed of important events in your students' lives.

Not all families have time to give to their child's school, but all parents and caregivers want a good education for their child. Show families that they are important and encourage them to participate, but do not make them feel judged if their time is limited. They will respond positively in any way they can. You, the families, and the students will all have a more enjoyable year as a result of the effort you put into keeping the lines of communication open.

Becoming a
Professional

» Professional development: You're not in it alone

As a culture, we are attached to the image of the inspiring teacher as a rugged individualist who has the innate ability to make students aware of their potential and lead them toward their dreams. We rarely think of these masterful teachers in collaboration and dialogue with their colleagues. Why? Perhaps it is due to the public perception that effective teaching is an intuitive gift rather than a craft that must be worked at and nurtured by other experienced teachers.

The fact is, the way most schools are structured, teaching can be an isolating profession. It is hard for teachers to find time to work and plan together. And given the many bureaucratic demands that teachers face in their day-to-day lives, it is not surprising that some of your colleagues will choose to close their doors and focus their energies on the one thing that ultimately matters, their students. Unfortunately, these conditions do not support the development of good teaching. If the teaching profession is to successfully challenge these conditions, then you, the future of the profession, must work with your more experienced colleagues to develop work habits that defy isolation, support collaboration, and drive effective teaching practice.

As a new teacher, you may have to deal with the isolation while juggling a very demanding work load. New faculty members are often given the most difficult classes to teach. If you are lucky, you will be provided with a curriculum guide, a teacher's edition of the course textbook, and a school handbook. More often than not, that is all the guidance you will receive. What other profession so effectively abandons its newest recruits?

The good news is, there is a lot you can do to break through the isolation. There are numerous organizations, and a growing number of schools and districts that recognize that supporting new teachers is critical to the future of the profession. Seek out opportunities to get help from more experienced teachers, and let their knowledge inform your practice. Many schools have formalized mentoring programs, but whether or not you find yourself in a situation where these mentoring supports are available, find colleagues whose opinions you respect and with whom you can share ideas. These informal collaborations are not only critical to the professional development of novice teachers like yourself, but play a significant role in helping more experienced teachers reflect on their own practice. In addition, informal collaboration often forms the backbone of powerful within-school networks that can support change and experimentation.

Find out what your school or district's approach to professional development is. Ask whether professional development opportunities are built into the regular teaching day. Is common planning time a priority? If it appears that professional development opportunities are poorly coordinated and unfocused, and there is limited support within the school, it is critical that you develop relations outside of the school that can provide you with the guidance and professional camaraderie you need. Professional groups and university programs are excellent places to find like-minded individuals who are interested in developing a critical approach to their practice. You should also subscribe to journals and utilize technology to expand the range of voices that can influence your teaching.

New teachers are often skeptical of teacher unions and associations, which are sometimes viewed as protectors of the status quo, but these organizations are critical to the developing professionalism of new teachers. From teacher centers, professional development laboratories, and discussion groups, to graduate-level courses, these organizations frequently offer a wide variety of programs that can support new teachers, especially those in unsupportive school settings.

School-level chapters of these organizations often spend considerable time addressing issues related to working conditions and compliance with collective bargaining agreements— issues that many new teachers prefer not to be involved with. But it is important that new teachers become active participants in the ongoing professional dialogue, as their energy can raise the level of discussion and help these organizations realize their progressive vision.

As a new teacher, you will want to strike a balance between fulfilling the specific demands of your teaching assignment and reflecting on the craft of teaching itself. Ideally, this type of reflection should be built into the culture of the school in which you work. If it is not, you must look to colleagues within and beyond your school for support.

» Find a mentor

The first few years of teaching are challenging years for virtually everyone who enters the profession. Having a mentor during this difficult period can greatly ease the stress, and help you through the missteps and tribulations that come with the territory. Mentoring is an opportunity to enter into a personal relationship with someone who can help you reflect on your practice and grow as a teacher. While it is provided formally in many school settings, you can also arrange for it on your own. Mentoring often revolves around a more experienced teacher giving a less experienced teacher advice. Ideally, the relationship should be non-evaluative and collegial rather than supervisorial, so that you feel comfortable experimenting as you look for the teaching techniques that work best for you and your students.

In a mentoring partnership, the mentor and the new teacher each have specific roles and responsibilities. If each does his/her part, mentoring can be a valuable growth experience for both. The following outline contains what we view as the primary responsibilities of each partner.

New Teacher's Responsibilities:
* Understand all of your classroom experiences as learning experiences.
* Seek out your mentor when you need help and be open to expressing failures as well as successes.

* Accept constructive criticism from your mentor and apply it to your teaching.
* Bear in mind that you are in the process of developing a teaching style/classroom persona with the goal of becoming the most effective and caring teacher you can be.

Mentor's Responsibilities:

* Be accessible on a daily basis.
* Guide the new teacher in finding his/her own teaching style and strategies.
* Help the new teacher develop classroom management strategies and consistent discipline.
* Assist the new teacher in creating a professional development plan, and make him/her aware of professional growth possibilities, e.g. institutes, workshops, conferences.
* Steer the new teacher through district and site policies and procedures.
* Guide the new teacher in developing a personal library of lesson plans and curriculum resources.

≫ Collaborate with colleagues

Mentoring is only one of many forms of collaboration that can enrich your professional experience and provide you with a wealth of new teaching ideas. What follows are descriptions of a few other forms of collaboration that experienced teachers have found useful and productive:

* Informally exchanging ideas and materials is probably the easiest, most natural way of getting to know your colleagues. You can start by mentioning something that went well in class, or by asking for feedback on a difficult situation. When you find another teacher whose approach you respect, see if you can exchange lessons or activities.

* Peer coaching, like mentoring, is an opportunity to get regular feedback on your teaching, improve instruction, and share best practices. Peer coaching usually occurs in groups of three or more teachers. It is important to set up your group carefully with people you feel comfortable getting feedback from. Do you want your conversations to be confidential? Lay out the ground rules before you begin. Peer coaching seems to be most effective when groups of teachers focus on specific goals. Simple questions like, "How can we do a better job of asking questions?" or, "Are we treating boys and girls differently in class?" can drive a group's conversations and activities.

* Case management is a fancy term for talking to and about individual students. The more you understand about your students' backgrounds, the better prepared you will be to meet their needs. Talking to colleagues about individual students can shed light on unique situations. It can alert you to medical conditions and family crises, and help you refine your instructional and interpersonal approaches. In addition, when students know that you care enough to talk about them outside of class, you contribute to a sense of school community and collective responsibility.

* As you grow as a teacher, initial concerns like classroom management, control, and how administrators perceive you may become secondary to questions of how students learn best. Every teacher knows that textbooks are only one component of the overall curriculum. One of

the most exciting parts of teaching is the opportunity to both organize information and create original ways of introducing it by formally writing curriculum. Working on curriculum with other teachers can help you develop lessons that address the needs of your students from a range of perspectives that you may not have considered otherwise. Any given lesson plan will improve through feedback from colleagues.

* Team teaching is another way for teachers to share ideas, but it involves working together with students in actual classes. Typically, team teachers have different levels of expertise in content areas, different instructional styles, and different relationships with their students, and negotiating roles can be very important. Will the partnership be equal or one-sided? Why? Who will be responsible for what work? When will planning occur? Team teaching can be extraordinarily rewarding. It does, however, require true dedication from its participants and support from those responsible for scheduling.

Whatever form of collaboration you choose to participate in, remember, teachers do not exist in a vacuum. For the more formal types of collaboration to be successful, you must court support from administrators. Administrators are generally eager to support practices that will increase student achievement and make them stand out among their peers. Approach administrators with a written plan after you have piloted and seen results from your collaboration. While you can continue to collaborate without administrative support, it is much more likely that your project will succeed in the long term if administrators are behind you.

Administrators can be particularly helpful with regard to two resources: time and space. You will have to be creative when it comes to finding time to collaborate. Possibilities include making time after school (ideally you could get paid out of a professional development fund); finding time during school (perhaps you could be released from other duties); or having the schedule reworked to enable common preparation periods or meeting times. It is also important to find an appropriate space for your collaborative work. Try to gain access to an empty classroom, part of the library, or any other reliable space where you can talk comfortably without having to attend to other pressing issues.

Finally, when you are meeting with your colleagues and great things are happening, keep records. Document your work. At some point, you might want to evaluate what started out rather informally. An evaluation may enable you to fine tune your collaboration, share ideas with others, develop your work in larger networks, or garner additional support.

>> Become A Change Agent

As a new teacher, you are learning as you go along how to organize time, plan, manage your classroom, and evaluate student work, while dealing with discipline problems, parents, and meetings. Under the circumstances, it is tempting to simply look the other way when you perceive that there is a problem in your class or school that you believe needs to be addressed by the administration. You may be afraid to discuss it with fellow teachers or administrators because you don't want to be labeled a troublemaker. You may also be afraid that the principal will think you are unhappy with the way the school is being run. Relax, you won't get into trouble. Change agents don't cause problems; they help find ways of solving them. The steps outlined below can help you address problems successfully without alienating your colleagues or administrators:

1. You perceive a problem in your school that you would like to see resolved.

2. Think deeply about the problem, and try to come up with as many possible solutions as you can.

3. Go to other teachers who you believe may share your concerns and talk to them about your ideas so they can see that you are serious about solving the problem and are not just dumping it in their laps without putting in any effort.

4. Establish a time to meet with like-minded teachers to mull over the problem. Study the problem and come up with solutions that you as a group can present to the principal. If it seems appropriate, write up a brief report—not more than two pages—outlining the problem and your group's suggestions.

5. Present your group's ideas to the principal. The principal will probably be happy to see a possible solution to a nagging problem. Because the group presented the issue as a school problem and not a principal problem, he or she will probably be pleased by your work.

Once you envision what kind of school you want to work in, you will feel compelled to try to help your own school move a little closer to that ideal. Keep your mind open to change, but do not try to do it alone. The secret of being a successful change agent is working with colleagues.

Join a Network

Networks are diverse in design and composition, ranging from relatively informal discussion and study groups among teachers, to cross-school and cross-district alliances of teachers and schools dedicated to professional growth or a particular area of intellectual and pedagogical exploration, to national organizations dedicated to an educational philosophy or program of action. However, despite their variety, educational networks share a common commitment to collaboration, sustained inquiry and reflection, and intellectual development and professional growth among their members. The teachers who authored this book are members of a national network called IMPACT II—The Teachers Network.

A personal history
by Jean Gibran

Throughout the years, Great Star taught my third graders how the Wampanoag people say thank you—taubut. Local artist Allan Rohan Crite told us about his long and creative life in our South End neighborhood. Poet Martin Espada shared what it was like to grow up bilingual. The class cooked plantains with Noemi's mother; Amanda's mother made an album with photos from our "Experience is Best" program; and we, with teachers and students from all over the city, researched and helped develop the first-ever Boston Women's Heritage Trail.

I wasn't always an activist. During my early teaching days, I followed a closed-door policy. In the teachers' room and during parents' nights, congeniality was my middle name. Parents and other "intruders" with appointments were welcomed. My students enjoyed their year-end field trip. But when I entered school, just minutes from downtown Boston, I closed the door on a wealth of commercial, cultural, and academic resources. When I entered my classroom, I closed the door on collegial, parental, and administrative talent.

Then I had an epiphany, thanks to the Boston Writing Project (BWP) at the University of Massachusetts. Two courses at BWP, an offshoot of the National Writing Project, University of California at Berkeley, persuaded me that young writers need the immediacy of personal experience. It was up to me to broaden our existential repertoires.

"Please...I'd rather do it myself!" was my motto for a while. Super-teaching meant research, making contacts, arranging classroom visits, and organizing pre-writing jaunts. I even dipped into personal funds for materials. I shudder when I remember weekends spent typing student stories for our classroom newsletter. No one respects a martyr. Another teacher set me straight: "Get outside help," she suggested. "Let older students and parents help with word processing." Then, computer literacy—mine and the kids—was in its infancy. Now, with software like the Amazing Writing Machine and contributing parents, student publishers have entered a new and prolific age. I look back with gratitude to that colleague who advised me to open my doors. Gradually, the following resource utilization model evolved. I call it "The Four C's":

1. COORDINATE curriculum objectives with business, state, and university institutions sponsoring teacher grants. The resulting cash flow underwrites the impossible bus trip and the occasional poetry reading. Bonding to the educational money market does involve proposal writing, but style and fluency improve with each venture. Caution: the grant-seeking route is time-consuming and highly competitive. Start small. My first ventures were often IMPACT II grants that gave me freedom to shop for materials. Gradually, I began to include fellow teachers and parents. Once "I" became "we," a strong school partnership evolved, leading the way for whole-school change. To learn more about going for the gold, contact: The Foundation Center, 79 Fifth Avenue, New York, NY 10003, (212) 620-4230, http://fdncenter.org, or access TeachNet (www.teachnet.org) and check out the "Let's Talk" section where grant opportunities are updated regularly.

2. COLLABORATE with groups that have already developed programs in specific interest areas. Why reinvent the wheel when volunteers, 4H agencies, museums, nature centers, and historical societies do it better? Does your wish list include regular classroom support? When a 20-year-old from Boston's City Year—funded by private industry and Americorps—worked with my students every morning for a year, our dreams for an organized 4-Square team, one-to-one tutoring, and even a school garden came true. Releasing the reins can mean some sacrifice of control, but saves endless planning hours. Representatives from outside organizations like to plan, so meetings with liaison personnel may require in-school working lunches or strategic conference calls. Collaboration may also involve some class field testing and observation. Exciting facilities like the Teachers' Resource Center at our local children's museum welcome parents, students, and teachers, and we, in turn, share operational space with their curriculum specialists. Reciprocity pays off. We once shared stories with a researcher studying collaborative writing, which yielded us a university-donated printer in a classic win-win trade-off.

3. COOPERATE with the entire school community. Teachers, students, parents, paraprofessionals, and administrators who set goals and work together toward the exploration of the outside world can eliminate the adversarial paralysis of "us versus them." Why should we ignore a knowledgeable administrator or curriculum expert from a different department? Resourceful teachers respect each other's talents. They also capitalize on cross-class/cross-school programs. Middle or high schoolers who regularly mentor younger peers develop useful insights on working with children; teachers bless the infusion of directed energy; and kids look up to their "big brothers and sisters." In-system wealth is our most valuable resource.

4. COMMUNICATE in a variety of ways with a variety of folk. A phone in every classroom should be our call in the new millennium. Along with improving parental dialogue, that line opens up endless possibilities: e-mail, distance learning, the Internet, and opportunities for teachers to "talk shop." For students, net pals are replacing pen pals. We live in a communication age where the other side of the world is just a key stroke away. Warning: virtual reality should not replace real world adventures. Students need to experience life on the outside, where interviewing the local tree warden or baker can jump-start a lifetime of learning.

≫ Getting the most mileage

Creative approaches to community organizations and local businesses can yield information and free materials, as well as funds. Banks and utility companies, environmental preservation groups, chambers of commerce, health care providers, and local performance groups are often willing to plan joint activities that can enrich your students' lives. Need carpeting for your reading center or file cabinets for your records? Donations of used or "outmoded" furnishings and equipment from small businesses or large corporations will enhance your classroom. Take advantage of recycling centers. Many school districts sponsor their own, while some industries and children's museums offer complimentary or low cost supplies. Increasingly popular are "shadow days" when students engaged in career planning have a chance to visit work sites and observe the typical professional work day. To learn more about how businesses or government can lend a hand, call public relations offices and ask to speak to a community relations manager.

Parent groups are priceless resources for teachers who do not live in the community where they teach. Also, neighborhood groups like local Crime Watches, the League of Women Voters, community gardens, day care and senior centers prepare visiting students for the rights and responsibilities of citizenship through community service learning.

Beyond-the-classroom experiences increase resources in a geometric progression. Wherever your destination, make sure students, parents, and administrators know that learning is the main objective. Provide ways for the class to document, articulate, and evaluate all stages of your excursions. If your school district does not have a list of recommended expeditions, work with the entire community and start your own annotated list. Throughout the country, computer databases are recording information on wide-ranging cultural opportunities. But nothing beats a human network of responsive educators eager to make a variety of experiences accessible to students.

Teacher centers bring new and experienced teachers together to explore teaching materials and techniques. They produce informative publications, offer in-service courses for teachers, and support educational excellence. A combination of library and laboratory, a teacher center can be located in a school, on a college campus, or in any one of many public and private facilities. Computer networks, with forums and bulletin boards, extend the scope and reach of the center concept and exponentially expand the resources of new teachers with access to modems.

HOW CAN YOU PREPARE YOURSELF FOR FUTURE ENTRY IN A COMPETITION OR GRANT OFFERING?

Start today to save artifacts of the best of your classroom projects and ideas:
  * Take photographs and videos of class activities.
  * Save examples of children's work and assessment samples.
Expose yourself to opportunities to improve, update, and expand your abilities as a teacher and as a learner:
  * Develop positive relationships with parents, students, and administrators. You may need to ask them for their written support, and they will need to be familiar with your work.
  * Attend professional development courses to keep up with "best practice" ideas in education.
  * Join professional organizations. This will keep you abreast of competitions and available grants and give you opportunities to network with other educators at yearly conventions.
  * Volunteer to make a presentation at a regional professional development workshop or convention. This will increase the visibility of your work, and you will become better known among the other teachers in your area.
  * Volunteer to serve on various committees in your school, if you are not already an active member of your educational community.
  * Become active in local community projects or groups. Look for ways to bring the community into your classroom and to bring your classroom into the community.

» Help and how to get it

Since the best classroom materials are not confined to the annual book order, getting your money's worth in the educational market depends on researching available programs, and comparison shopping. Buying into local and national groups, which may or may not charge for membership and/or subscriptions, means first retrieving and reviewing free brochures, directories, catalogs, and bibliographies. It pays if informed colleagues share the search, the sources, and the resulting purchases. Whether the resource is a curriculum guide, an article, or a program of activities, the discriminating shopper relies on instinct and passion for a subject, considers students' needs and interests, and incorporates the school's stated curriculum. If you are reading this book, you are probably on your way to being not only a teacher who employs a vast array of resources but also one who will soon have much to contribute for the pleasure, enlightenment, and success of other teachers. As a first step in accessing our nation's great and endless educational resources and grant opportunities, write, call, or e-mail the following organizations (they may also have branches in your community):

American Association of Museums
1575 Eye Street N.W., Suite 400
Washington D.C. 20005
(202) 289-9127
www.aam-us.org
〉 for a catalog listing all children's museums, science museums; the *Official Museum Directory* is available in most libraries

American Educator
Center for Civic Education
We the People...
5146 Douglas Fir Road
Calabasas, CA 91302
(818) 591-9321
www.civiced.org
〉 for this federally funded program's brochure on complimentary elementary, middle, and high school texts that reflect national standards for civics and government

American Federation of Teachers
555 New Jersey Avenue N.W.
Washington D.C. 20001
(202) 879-4400
www.aft.org

〉 for a free catalog of publications and the members' magazine

Cooperative Extensions
Contact your state university for site location.
〉 4H youth development programs are located in counties across the U.S. and are part of the cooperative extension programs of all land grant or state universities

Educational Resources
Information Center (ERIC)
Clearing House on Urban Education
Teachers College/Columbia University
Box 40
New York, NY 10027
(212) 678-3433
http://ericeece.org
〉 for ERIC Ready Reference #6, listing clearinghouses, with complete addresses and brief descriptions; for interactive AskERIC, an Internet-based information service

Department of Veterans Affairs
Office of Public Affairs 80D
810 Vermont Avenue N.W.
Washington D.C. 20420
(202) 273-5771
www.va.gov
〉 for free literature on celebrating America's freedom

IMPACT II—The Teachers Network
285 West Broadway, Suite 540
New York, NY 10013
(212) 966-5582
www.teachnet.org
〉 for copies of IMPACT II's newsletter, the *IMPACT II Star***, and other IMPACT II publications including the *Teachers Guide to Cyberspace* ($19.95); for access to TeachNet, a primary Internet source for new ideas and lesson plans by teachers, for teachers

League of Women Voters
1730 M Street N.W.
Washington D.C. 20036-4508
(202) 429-1965
www.lwv.org
〉 for information on voter registration and a Get Out and Vote! kit ($15)

National Education Association
1201 Sixteenth Street N.W.
Washington D.C. 20036
(202) 833-4000
www.nea.org
❭ for access to departments offering
research services and communications,
and the monthly newspaper, *NEA Today*

National Geographic Society
Educational Services
PO Box 10597
Des Moines, IA 50340-0597
(800) 368-2728
www.nationalgeographic.com
❭ for a brochure on videos for
students K-12 and information on
interactive geography projects

National School-to-Work Learning &
Information Center
400 Virginia Avenue S.W. Room 150
Washington D.C. 20024
(800) 251-7236
http://stw.ed.gov
❭ for information on practical tools for
the classroom, school-to-work resource
library, and resource bulletins

National Wildlife Federation
8925 Leesburg Pike
Vienna, VA 22184
(703) 790-4000
www.nwf.org
❭ for information on programs including:
Backyard Wildlife Habitat Program,
International School Grounds Day,
Animals Tracks Hotline; for information
on publications including: *Your Big
Backyard*, *Ranger Rick*, *National Wildlife*,
and *Conservation Directory*

National Women's History Project
7738 Bell Road
Windsor, CA 95492
(707) 838-6000
www.nwhp.org

❭ for a catalog on literature and
classroom activities featuring
women's contributions

National Writing Project
5511 Tolman Hall #1670
School of Education
University of California
Berkeley, CA 94720-1670
(510) 642-0963
www.gse.berkeley.edu/research/
nwp/nwp.html
❭ for a brochure on writing sites
nationwide; annual special associate
membership ($20) includes *The
Quarterly* and *The Voice*

Peace Corps
1990 K Street N.W.
Washington D.C. 20526
(202) 606-3360
www.peacecorps.gov
❭ for information on teacher
programs and Worldwise Schools

Polaroid Education Program
565-3 Technology Square
Cambridge, MA 02139
(781) 386-5090
www.polaroid.com
❭ for a brochure on workshops (with
curriculum materials and camera) on
visual learning in the classroom

SerVermont
P.O. Box 516
Chester, VT 05143
(802) 875-2278
❭ for student community
service learning material

Smithsonian Institution
Office of Elementary and
Secondary Education
Arts and Industry Building
Room 1163
900 Jefferson Drive S.W.
Washington D.C. 20560

(202) 357-2425
www.si.edu
❭ for information on museums,
activities, tours, and publications
(an online *Resource Guide for Teachers*
can be downloaded off the web site;
a print copy is $5)

Southern Poverty Law Center
Teaching Tolerance
400 Washington Avenue
Montgomery, AL 36104
(334) 264-0286
www.splcenter.org
❭ for free magazine and video-texts
addressing themes of diversity,
respect, and conflict resolution

Teachers of English to Speakers
of Other Languages Inc.
1600 Cameron St., Suite 300
Alexandria, VA 22314-2751
(703) 836-0774
www.tesol.edu
❭ for a free *Access* brochure to evaluate
programs for language-minority students

The Annenberg/CPB Projects
Attn: Learner Online
901 E Street N.W.
Washington D.C. 20004
(202) 879-9600
www.learner.org/aboutacpb
❭ for information on *Journey
North*, *French in Action*, and
science and math initiatives

The U.S. Department of Education
600 Independence Avenue S.W.
Washington D.C. 20202-0498
(800) USA-LEARN
www.ed.gov
❭ for wide ranging publications,
projects, resource directories

U.S. Environmental Protection Agency
Office of Community and
Intergovernmental Relations
Public Information Center
401 M Street S.W.
Washington D.C. 20460
(202) 260-2090
www.epa.gov/epahome
〉 for youth publications and information
on guides, curricula, and grants

WGBH Educational Print and Outreach
125 Western Avenue
Boston, MA 02134
(617) 492-2777
〉 for free biannual curriculum guides on
the following PBS programs: *Nova,
Science Odyssey*, and *Carmen San Diego*

PROFESSIONAL ORGANIZATIONS
YOU MAY WANT TO JOIN

American Alliance of Health, Physical
Education, Recreation and Dance
1900 Association Drive
Reston, VA 20191
(800) 213-7193
www.aahperd.org

Council for Exceptional Children
1920 Association Drive
Reston, VA 20191
(888) CEC-SPED
www.cec.sped.org

International Reading Association
800 Barksdale Road
P.O. Box 8139
Newark, DE 19714
(302) 731-1600
www.reading.org

National Association for
Bilingual Education
1220 L Street N.W., Suite 605
Washington D.C. 20005
(202) 898-1829
www.nabe.org

National Association for the
Education of Young Children
1509 16th Street N.W.
Washington D.C. 20036-1426
(202) 328-2614
www.naeyc.org

National Council for Accreditation
of Teacher Education
2010 Massachusetts Avenue N.W.
Suite 500
Washington D.C. 20036-1023
(202) 466-7496
www.ncate.org

National Council for the
Social Studies
3501 Newark Street N.W.
Washington D.C. 20016
(202) 966-7840
www.ncss.org

National Council of
Teachers of English
1111 West Kenyon Road
Urbana, IL 61801
(800) 369-6283
www.ncte.org

National Council of Teachers
of Mathematics
1906 Association Drive
Reston, VA 20191
(703) 620-9840
www.nctm.org

National Science Teachers
Association
1840 Wilson Blvd.
Arlington, VA 22201-3000
(703) 243-7100
www.nsta.org

National Society for
Experiential Education
3509 Haworth Drive, Suite 207
Raleigh, NC 27609-7229
(919) 787-3263
www.nsee.org

You may want to subscribe to these publications:

Art Education, Educational Leadership, Education Week, Teaching Children Mathematics, Teacher Magazine, Instructor, Learning, Smithsonian, Natural History, Phi Delta Kappan for teachers; and for children, *Calliope* (World History), *Cobblestones* (American History), *Cricket* (Literature), *Highlights* (Activities and Stories), *Muse* (Science), *Odyssey* (astronomy and space), *Ranger Rick* (Natural History), *Stone Soup,* and *Young Authors* (student writing).

These are just the tip of the periodical iceberg. With all the choices, the right publication is out there. Before subscribing, do a library search and find out about offers of sample issues or free subscriptions. Most magazines are on the Internet too! The proliferation of great web sites and voluminous archives offer a great deal of valuable information on publications for you and your kids.

THE INTERVIEW: SUCCESSFUL STRATEGIES FOR STUDENTS

1. Be prepared. Research your subjects before the interview. If you plan to use recording devices—cameras, tape recorders, videos—be sure to ask permission. Know your equipment, and check it before and during your talk.

2. Establish a friendly atmosphere.

3. Use a strong clear voice. Remember, you must reach the whole group.

4. Possible questions to ask:
— What is your job? Could you describe it briefly?
— How did you choose your job?
— What are some advantages of your line of work?
— What are some disadvantages of your line of work?
— What is the salary range—the average beginning and ending salary?
— What are some other career possibilities related to your job?
— What is the future for your line of work?

5. Concerning the establishment:
— What is the history of this establishment?
— What is its importance in the community or business world?
— What are its future plans?

6. Continue the interview with other relevant questions.

7. After your interview, review and organize your notes. Plan ways to share the results with the school community. While your data is still fresh, write it up along with pertinent observations and background material.

8. Follow up the experience with a thank you letter and send a copy of your report or publishing efforts to your subject.

Resources on Resources

Look around and you will find a wealth of resources in your community, usually only a phone call away. The following literature may help:

Basile, Carole G. and Collins, Fred. *Nature at Your Doorstep: Real World Investigations for Primary Students*. Grades K-3. Teacher Ideas Press, 1997. Ten units connect children with their environment. This systemic approach to several nature topics includes lesson plans and reproducible data sheets, along with ways to integrate science, mathematics, and language arts experiences.

Hollenbeck, Kathleen M. *Exploring Our World: Neighborhoods and Communities*. Grades 1-3. Scholastic Inc, 1997. Incorporating learning-center and literature links, this book provides solid ideas and hands-on materials for teachers who like to get up and go.

✔ Resource checklist

Teachers are busy people, and quite often they find themselves too busy to investigate how they can bring into their classrooms additional resources that would enhance their teaching and add variety and interest to the curriculum. Many of these resources are quite close at hand and easy to obtain. Some easy-to-find resources available in your community are listed here—and maybe this list will get you thinking about some that have been overlooked:

- ☐ Newspapers.
- ☐ Diaries—check local historical societies and museums.
- ☐ Journals—check your local colleges or university.
- ☐ Government documents—library reference is helpful here.
- ☐ Photographs—libraries and, again, museums are good resources.
- ☐ Artwork—museums of art.
- ☐ Letters.
- ☐ Artifacts—museums of natural history.
- ☐ Periodicals.
- ☐ Newsletters.
- ☐ Special reviews—check special groups or societies.
- ☐ Historical society.
- ☐ Chamber of commerce—often has lists of businesses that are resources to teachers.
- ☐ Art museum, historical museum—offer tours and have trained docents available to interpret programs to students. Many museums have outreach programs and will send docents into classrooms.
- ☐ Local societies like the Audubon Society and the Humane Society—offer resources such as films, speakers, and curriculum materials for all grade levels.
- ☐ County courthouse—offers a law tour led by a trained docent, as well as a mock trial suitable for students in the upper grades.
- ☐ Park rangers and environmental groups such as the Sierra Club.
- ☐ Local utility companies, such as the gas, electric, and telephone companies—offer a list of free films, speakers, and units on special topics such as energy conservation.
- ☐ Major oil companies—offer tours, some of their offshore platforms.
- ☐ Local zoo—sends out curriculum materials; offers tours with trained guides.
- ☐ Local businesses—are often involved in partnerships with schools, and are valuable resources to teachers. Check with your local industry education council or chamber of commerce.
- ☐ Speakers bureaus at junior colleges and universities—offer speakers for all grade levels and in many subject areas. Call their offices of public information.
- ☐ County parks—often have naturalists and sometimes geologists on staff. Check to see what they offer to teachers.

On Foolish Dreams and Teaching Kids

by Cynthia Carbone Ward

I began my teaching career at the age of 43. I was still grieving over the recent death of a brother, and I wanted to do something constructive and hopeful in his memory. I viewed teaching as a noble calling, perhaps because I was lucky enough to have had one or two teachers in my own life who had filled me with a sense of possibility.

I thought of my 11th grade history teacher, Mr. Sexton, a man as often the object of furtive derision as grudging respect. Like all school teachers, he possessed eccentricities of behavior and appearance that generated cruel nicknames and set him apart from normal human beings—but this was standard. One rainy day in June of 1967, he brought out a record player and had us listen to "The Impossible Dream" from *Man of La Mancha*, which at the time was a Broadway hit. As the music played, we silently read the lyrics from the purple-inked mimeographed sheets he had distributed.

At one point I looked up and saw that Mr. Sexton had tears in his eyes. It was embarrassing. It cut too close. I knew that he saw this song as an inspiring creed by which to live our lives; its lyrics were his gift to us, a parting message. But I did not wish to contemplate Mr. Sexton's personal dreams and vulnerability, nor could I ever admit that this schmaltz affected me as well. I lowered my gaze and never said a word. But I never forgot it, either.

Today, as a middle school teacher, I know very well how Mr. Sexton must have felt alone in his classroom after the bell. There are many days when I simply don't think I am getting through, no matter how much I give. Just as it was in 1967, the facade of coolness is the ubiquitous mask of adolescence. And one of the things a teacher has to learn is that you don't always know who you are reaching, or even when the message will arrive. But you must keep trying—for you are the knight of the impossible dream, and shining idealism must be your armor.

Even when we do not feel brave or hopeful, those of us who are teachers, or parents, for that matter, are morally obligated to act in brave and hopeful ways. If our house is flooded, and all that we possess is a thimble, then thimble by thimble we must begin to empty the water. We must demonstrate our own conviction that in time the task will be accomplished, and we must prove our willingness to labor towards that end. What's more, we must show those within our reach how to cup their hands and help.

I will be honest. At times I have looked at students and asked myself who these aliens are. Maybe it comes of starting a career at middle-age. For my entire first year, I wondered what had become of discipline and respect. I yearned to foster constructive social action. I was troubled by self-centered rudeness and indifference to the pain of others. "They're only kids," people said, "you have to meet them on their own terms."

For a time, I accepted this. But eventually I came to my senses. Their terms? Will the world meet them on their terms? Are there not values and rules of conduct that they must adopt? I realized it was up to me to model responsible adult behavior, hold kids accountable for their actions, and broaden their sphere of awareness and responsibility. Particularly among middle school students, who wander in that strange border country called adolescence, a sense of moral direction is essential. And it isn't implicitly learned through the basic curriculum. I found a like-minded colleague, Jennifer Levin, and we launched a virtual jihad.

Teaching is an act of supreme defiance against apathy and cynicism. And to strip it of its moral component is to render it without a soul. At the beginning of school, we took our class to the Museum of Tolerance in Los Angeles. Students were confronted with images and voices of the Holocaust, a time not so far removed from the present. "Evil persists when good people do nothing." We saw what evil looks like, what indifference sustains. It was quite a jolt.

But we cannot simply get depressed about it. Depression is self-indulgent. One must use the fuel of sadness and anger to build a fire that warms. We required our students to find tangible ways to make the world a better place. They visited homeless children, collected canned goods, raised money for Habitat for Humanity. They learned that they each have the power to mitigate the world's collective misery.

Because of the nature of our world, it was all too easy to find examples of intolerance and suffering throughout the social studies curriculum. We also looked for the people in history who stood up for what was right. Students wrote about times in their own lives when they had done the right thing. They created children's books with moral themes. I found that moral courage is a concept that students had not consciously explored, nor is it a principle that can simply be preached. Moral courage and decency must be modeled by the significant adults in a child's life. As a teacher I must be particularly aware of the behaviors I demonstrate, whether it means containing my anger or giving it a righteous voice.

Jennifer and I also emphasized the small civilities that make life more pleasant. We taught manners, using sometimes comical role-playing, and culminating in an "etiquette dinner" in which our classroom was transformed into an elegant restaurant. Students learned that the purpose of manners is to make people more comfortable. "It hurts my feelings when you walk in and don't say good morning to me," I confessed. I am no longer invisible. They humor me, at least.

I stealthily monitored many interactions outside of the classroom, as well. "You have no right to butt in!" said one indignant student. But butting in is a teacher's duty. One cannot teach character if one is bent on being popular or cool. I have called kids on meanness, tactlessness, even just plain old foul language, which I simply feel loses its power from overuse, has a generally corrosive effect, and is a rather flaccid and uncreative way to express oneself.

We often took the pathway of poetry, for it leads directly to the heart. The students wrote poems about their adolescent pain; Jennifer and I dug up some awful poetry we ourselves had written, and we sat in a circle on the floor and shared these. We discovered that we were all more alike than different. We could empathize with one another, be a little gentler, perhaps.

I thought it was a good year, but Jennifer and I drew up student questionnaires to help us assess its impact. The first part consisted of a series of hypothetical situations. Students were asked to write down what they thought they should do, and what they actually would do in each situation. Some of the responses were inadvertently funny:

Your friend asks if he can copy your homework. What would you do?
I would normally say I did not do it neither.

Someone at school is always sitting alone at lunch. What would you do?
I would probably ignore him too but I would feel sorry for him.

Many of the responses revealed that students would not necessarily do what they knew they should do. I was disappointed at first, but then felt gratitude for their honesty. In fact, their answers indicated that they were really thinking about each situation, that they were at least aware of values and moral principles upon which to base their reactions, and finally, that they were not going to simply "snow" their teachers with the answers they thought we wanted. I saw this as a good thing.

Besides, these kids don't know what will and will not affect them, any more than I knew in 1967 that I would someday be influenced by Mr. Sexton's tears. I believe in the retroactive nature of learning. Today I am planting seeds that may lie dormant for years, then flower unexpectedly in the rain and sun of the future.

In the second part of the questionnaire, students were to write an open-ended essay about how the class had changed them, if at all. Almost everyone mentioned pride about having done community service, a greater awareness of prejudice and intolerance, and the fact that they now treated people with more politeness. No one waxed poetic, no one claimed that his/her life had been significantly altered, no one was inspired to change the world, or even become a teacher. A few admitted they did not really know what the effect of all this had been. And one student wrote, "I did not get anything out of this class because the teachers did not seem to realize that this is reality and we can't become color blind with the flick of a switch..." He's the one who convinced me to keep going.

Notice how I have turned negatives into positives. I ignore all the reasons to stop and find only reasons to continue. I believe in the hope, even when it is a lie. I teach because although I know that "this is reality," I will never accept that it must be so, and I find it particularly unacceptable that a 13-year-old boy does. I go forth to battle windmills, injustice, or simply ennui. To teach is to head a revolution every day.

 74

ABOUT IMPACT II–THE TEACHERS NETWORK

IMPACT II—The Teachers Network is a nationwide, educational non-profit organization that supports innovative teachers who exemplify professionalism, independence, and creativity within public school systems.

HOW IT WORKS
It begins with a teacher's good idea. Through small grants, IMPACT II—The Teachers Network helps the teacher package that innovation; connects that teacher with interested colleagues; and then recruits all interested teachers into a continuing professional and social network.

THE BETTER IDEA
Anyone who is any good at any job figures out ways to do it better. IMPACT II-The Teachers Network designates teachers or teams of teachers who have developed better projects for their own classrooms as "disseminators" and then awards them grants averaging $500.

PACKAGING THE IDEA
Teachers use the grant money to package their ideas and to connect with other interested teachers, known as "adaptors," who receive grants to cut and fit the original ideas to their classrooms. The disseminator teacher wants to help others improve their work; the adaptors want to make their own classrooms better.

CONNECTING GOOD PEOPLE
Because teacher-to-teacher teaching and learning does not happen magically, IMPACT II—The Teachers Network manages the process. Those innovative faculty members—disseminators and adaptors—are recruited into a professional and social network of like-minded individuals.

WHY IT WORKS
IMPACT II—The Teachers Network was founded in 1979, and had the results of its first evaluation in 1982. Dedicated to self-improvement, IMPACT II—The Teachers Network has an extensive database covering its outcomes. Survey questions originally asked in 1981 were revisited in 1992-93. The survey showed that after 10 years, the main effects of IMPACT II—The Teachers Network remain strongly in place.

THE TEACHERS NETWORK
* recognizes outstanding teachers
* improves classroom instruction
* improves diverse sites
* provides lasting effects
* connects outstanding teachers
* disseminates good ideas
* keeps good teachers in teaching

WHERE IT WORKS
IMPACT II—The Teachers Network model has been adopted by large urban school districts, entire states, consortiums of suburban and rural school districts, and educational foundations.

Over 30,000 teachers participate in IMPACT II—The Teachers Network nationwide. These professionals have reached out to another 500,000 teachers, using IMPACT II—The Teachers Network's research-documented, teacher-to-teacher development techniques.

THE TEACHERS VOICE INITIATIVE
Ten years after its founding, in 1989, when the President held an education summit and did not invite a single classroom teacher, IMPACT II—The Teachers Network launched its Teachers Voice Initiative. Landmark projects include:

* Inventing the Future of Teaching (WWOR-TV, 1989)
* The First Institute for the Future of Education (Snowbird, UT, 1990)
* *The Teachers' Vision of the Future of Education: A Challenge to the Nation* (published 1991)
* The Second Institute for the Future of Education (Snowbird, UT, 1992)
* The First National Teachers Summit (Miami, FL, 1993)
* The Teachers Network (televised coast-to-coast, 1994)
* The Third Institute for the Future of Education (Snowbird, UT, 1994)
* Nationwide Teacher Leadership Project (founded 1995)
* The First Teacher Policy Institute (New York City, 1995-96)
* National Teacher Policy Institute (founded 1996)

HANDBOOKS BY TEACHERS, FOR TEACHERS
IMPACT II—The Teachers Network publishes handbooks that are written *by teachers, for teachers.* Titles in this series include:

* *New Teachers Handbook*
* *Teachers Guide to Cyberspace*
* *How We Are Changing Schools Collaboratively*
* *How Teachers Are Changing Schools*
* *Teacher/Parent Partnerships Handbook*
* *Experienced Teachers Handbook*

IMPACT II—The Teachers Network also produces a series of videotapes, and publishes a newsletter, the *IMPACT II Star**,* and occasional reports, including "Changing Schools, Changing Roles— Redefining the Role of the Principal in a Restructured School."

TEACHNET
TeachNet, IMPACT II—The Teachers Network's web site, features daily classroom specials; a searchable database of over 500 teacher-developed, student-centered, award-winning projects; and bulletin boards on teacher leadership, educational policymaking, and funding opportunities.

For more information contact:
IMPACT II—The Teachers Network
285 West Broadway, Suite 540
New York, NY 10013-2272
(212) 966-5582 tel.
(212) 941-1787 fax
e-mail: teachnet@teachnet.org
http://www.teachnet.org

IMPACT II SITE INFORMATION

Contra Costa County (CA)
Sandy Bruketta,
sbruketta@cccoe.k12.ca.us
Student Programs Department
Contra Costa County Office of
Education
77 Santa Barbara Road
Pleasant Hill, CA 94523

Los Angeles (CA)
Dianne Glinos,
dglinos@laedu.lalc.k12.ca.us
Los Angeles Educational Partnership
315 West Ninth Street, Suite 1110
Los Angeles, CA 90015

Santa Barbara County (CA)
Nancy Emerson,
nemerson@ceo.scceo.k12.ca.us
IMPACT II
Santa Barbara County Education Office
4400 Cathedral Oaks Road
Santa Barbara, CA 93160-6307

Ventura County (CA)
Kerry Roscoe
IMPACT II Coordinator
VCSS, Educational Services Center
570 Airport Way
Camarillo, CA 93010

Colorado, Kansas, New Mexico,
Oklahoma, Texas, and Wyoming
Carol Shearon,
cshearon@msp.psco.com
Program Manager
New Century Energies Foundation
1225 17th Street, Suite 2000
Denver, CO 80202-5533

State of Connecticut
Bill Farr
Celebration of Excellence
205 Skiff Street
Hamden, CT 06517-1095

Dade County (FL)
Linda Lecht, dpef@aol.com
Executive Director
Dade Public Education Fund
4299 N.W. 36th Street, Suite 203
Miami, FL 33166

Broward County (FL)
Kim Bentley, Executive Director
CoCo Burns, Program Coordinator
Broward Educational Foundation, Inc.
600 S.E. 3rd Avenue, 8th Floor
Ft. Lauderdale, FL 33301

State of Illinois
Michele Micetich, micetich@imsa.edu
Michelle Adams, adams@imsa.edu
System for Partnership Initiatives
Illinois Mathematics & Science Academy
1500 West Sullivan Road
Aurora, IL 60506-1000

Chicago (IL)
Jennifer Gwilliam, gwilliamjb@aol.com
Chicago Foundation for Education
400 N. Michigan Avenue, Room 311
Chicago, IL 60610

Fayette County (KY)
Christy Hogan, mchogan@aol.com
Program Director
Ambrose Building
Fayette County Public Schools
701 East Main Street
Lexington, KY 40502

Baton Rouge (LA)
Jan Melton
Academic Distinction Fund
8550 United Plaza Boulevard, Suite 204
Baton Rouge, LA 70809

State of Maine
Jenifer Van Deusen, jenifer_van
deusen@melink.avcnet.org
Maine Center for Educational Services
292 Court Street, P.O. Box 620
Auburn, ME 04212

Baltimore (MD)
Drue Whitney
Director
Teacher Effectiveness Programs
Fund for Educational Excellence
800 North Charles Street #450
Baltimore, MD 21201

Boston (MA)
Barbara Locurto,
blocurto@boston.k12.ma.us
Director, IMPACT II
55 New Dudley Street, Bldg. 1
Boston, MA 02120

National Peace Corps Association
Anne Baker, rpcvgtn@aol.com
Director, Global TeachNet
1900 L Street, N.W., #205
Washington, DC 20036

State of New Jersey
Joyce Kersey, apluskid@ix.netcom.com
Executive Director
A+ For Kids Teacher Network
2 Village Boulevard, Second Floor
Forrestal Village
Princeton, NJ 08540

New York City (NY)
Rafael Ortiz, rortiz@teachnet.org
IMPACT II
285 West Broadway, Suite 540
New York, NY 10013

Central New York
Patti Galini, pgalini@dreamscape.net
Central New York Teaching Center
4860 Onondaga Road
Syracuse, NY 13215

Westchester County (NY)
Elissa Spedafino,
espedafi@westplaza.lhric.org
IMPACT II
SW BOCES
2 Westchester Plaza
Elmsford, NY 10523

Chapel Hill-Carrboro (NC)
Hazel Gibbs, hgibbs@chccs.k12.nc.us
Personnel Director
Chapel Hill-Carrboro City Schools
Lincoln Center, Merritt Mill Road
Chapel Hill, NC 27516

Portland (OR)
Sandy Rosenfeld, rosenfelds@aol.com
Portland Association of Teachers
345 NE 8th Street
Portland, OR 97232-2708

Houston (TX)
Dr. Susan Wethington, sweth@tenet.edu
Achievement Institute
IMPACT II Office
3830 Richmond Avenue
Houston, TX 77027

Fairfax County (VA)
Sylvia Auton,
sauton@walnuthill.fcsp.k12.va.us
Betty Costello, betty4578@aol.com
James Dallas,
jdallas@walnuthill.fcsp.k12.va.us
IMPACT II
Fairfax County Public Schools
7423 Camp Alger Avenue
Falls Church, VA 22042

National Headquarters
IMPACT II—The Teachers Network
285 West Broadway, Suite 540
New York, NY 10013-2272
Ellen Dempsey, President
Ellen Meyers, Vice-President—
Programs and Communications
Rafael Ortiz, Director of Technical
Assistance and Development

INDEX